"Joining God's dream for our neighborh clarion call of racial justice and reconcili versations about race haven't included place, and vice versa. With the in-sight of a scholar and wisdom that only comes from putting ideas into practice, Dr. Leong offers an invitation to the belonging, solidarity, and hope we so desperately need today. If you believe we need each other, you need this book. If you don't believe we need each other, you need this book. I'm so grateful for this timely contribution."

Tim Soerens, cofounding director, The Parish Collective, coauthor of *The New Parish*

"Race is neither a white/black issue nor is it merely one of political correctness. Rather, it's about ghettos, ethnic enclaves, suburbia, and gentrification. David Leong helps us see how racialized our cities have been historically and how we continue to suffer under these decisions from decades ago. But *Race and Place* also provides us with concrete steps to live out the good news of justice and shalom in our neighborhoods and communities. There is plenty here for theorists to mull over and much for activists to work for as well."

Amos Yong, professor of theology and mission, Fuller Theological Seminary

"Place matters. *Race and Place* adds to our understanding about race by showing us that this dialog does not happen in a vacuum but in geographic places and spaces. Jesus came to break down the dividing walls between us. It is in specific locations we work out what it means to walk through those dividing walls."

Jude Tiersma Watson, associate professor of urban mission, Fuller Seminary

RACE & PLACE

How Urban Geography Shapes the Journey to Reconciliation

David P. Leong

Foreword by Soong-Chan Rah

An imprint of InterVarsity Press
Downers Grove, Illinois

InterVarsity Press
P.O. Box 1400, Downers Grove, IL 60515-1426
ivpress.com
email@ivpress.com

InterVarsity Press® is the book-publishing division of InterVarsity Christian Fellowship/USA®, a movement of students and faculty active on campus at hundreds of universities, colleges, and schools of nursing in the United States of America, and a member movement of the International Fellowship of Evangelical Students. For information about local and regional activities, visit intervarsity.org.

Cover design: Cindy Kiple
Interior design: Beth McGill
Images: abstract NYC art: ©littleny/iStockphoto
turn right sign: ©jojoo64/iStockphoto

ISBN 978-0-8308-4134-9 (print)
ISBN 978-0-8308-8102-4 (digital)

Printed in the United States of America ♾

As a member of the Green Press Initiative, InterVarsity Press is committed to protecting the environment and to the responsible use of natural resources. To learn more, visit greenpressinitiative.org.

Library of Congress Cataloging-in-Publication Data

Names: Leong, David P. (David Paul), author.
Title: Race and place : how urban geography shapes the journey to reconciliation / David P. Leong.
Description: Downers Grove : InterVarsity Press, 2017. | Includes bibliographical references and index.
Identifiers: LCCN 2016046181 (print) | LCCN 2016046927 (ebook) | ISBN 9780830841349 (pbk. : alk. paper) | ISBN 9780830881024 (eBook)
Subjects: LCSH: Cities and towns—Religious aspects—Christianity. | Christianity and geography. | Reconciliation--Religious aspects—Christianity.
Classification: LCC BR115.C45 L46 2017 (print) | LCC BR115.C45 (ebook) | DDC 234/.5—dc23
LC record available at https://lccn.loc.gov/2016046181.

P 20 19 18 17 16 15 14 13 12 11 10 9 8 7 6 5 4 3 2 1
Y 34 33 32 31 30 29 28 27 26 25 24 23 22 21 20 19 18 17

To Chris, Jonas, and Micah,

who keep my feet on the ground

and my eyes on the horizon.

Contents

Foreword

Soong-Chan Rah

As a kid growing up in an inner-city neighborhood in Baltimore, I learned very early the importance of geography. You knew there were certain boundaries and geographic markers that you did not cross. The cemetery was off limits—that's where all the beat downs occurred. You either walked around that geographic boundary or you learned to run real fast. The urban neighborhood of my elementary and middle school years included poor blacks, poor whites, and poor Korean immigrants. We all lived in the same apartment complex, attended the same middle school, and shared the common experience of poverty. Yet despite our proximity and our commonality, the neighborhood was starkly divided along racial lines. Shared space did not yield shared lives.

During my high school years, my family lived in a middle-class suburban neighborhood. The planned community of this neighborhood offered a different type of geography but seemingly the same type of separation. Different patterns of life, connections, and relationships were pursued in the suburbs vis-à-vis the city, but the same results emerged. Ironically, in a planned neighborhood built with the intention of generating a happy community, the same narrative from my inner-city neighborhood remained: shared space did not yield shared lives.

Over the last several decades, I have sought to better understand how race relations in America have impacted and shaped US social history. I have sought to better understand how the formation of a dysfunctional social imagination has created a wounded church and a broken society. I have sought to better understand how biblical justice intersects with the reality of injustice in our world. And I have come to the conclusion that the pursuit of biblical justice in the United States requires the uncomfortable, painful, and even polarizing pursuit of racial justice.

However, this high-stakes conversation, and its dealings with the whole spectrum of racial justice that understands the social-historical context of American society, is exhausting work. Those of us who have been in the fight grow weary from the ongoing process of explanation, particularly for people of color who constantly explain, from a myriad of angles, with their explanations and analysis oftentimes falling on deaf years. Ed Gilbreath said it best when he described the concept of "racial fatigue."

In recent years, there has been a resurgence of interest by American Christians in the biblical call to justice ministry. However, this interest has not always yielded a deeper engagement in the hard work needed to *enact* biblical justice. A closer look at the fad of urban ministry reveals our error, for without rigorous cultural exegesis and social analysis, those who move to the city to be urban missionaries are simply urban colonizers. This reminds us that ministry in the complex geography of American society can never be understood in a vacuum. It must be understood in the full range of complexity. This book offers a way into that complexity.

To change the social imagination of a community, a church, a denomination, and even a nation requires hard work. For those who are just beginning their journey toward biblical racial justice, this book offers an important primer. For those who have grown weary of trying to explain the reality of injustice in the world, this book offers markers and guideposts to persevere in that conversation. I am so grateful for David Leong's fresh and unique look at race in America. I will "never look at another freeway, public school, or suburban home the same way again." The book offers the needed work of cultural and social exegesis and also offers the potential positive power of the Christian imagination. Allow David Leong—a scholar, a pastor, an urbanite, a deeply spiritual and thoughtful follower of Jesus—to guide you through this important theological journey.

Introduction

Street Signs and Color Lines

With all the distracted drivers on our roads these days, it seems a fitting reminder to pay attention to our surroundings. For example, it's important to read street signs—"slow down," "children present," "school zone," "construction ahead," and so forth. These kinds of street signs are obvious and provide pertinent information. But there are also other kinds of signs on our streets, some less obvious, but no less important. In fact, many of the signs most deserving of our attention take various forms, and some of the most meaningful signs are the ones we may not see as signs at all.[1] Rather, they are "signs of the times," whether complex cultural texts or the prophetic signs Jesus speaks of in Matthew 16:3.

In our cities today, one sign of the times is that our streets have been burning, both literally and figuratively. From Ferguson to Baltimore, and many places in between, the fires of racial unrest have once again erupted in urban communities that have historically faced cycles of generational poverty and structural inequalities. Some of us have been burned by these injustices, while others have simply watched from a distance in confusion or disbelief. I believe that our understanding of these street signs depends largely on our geography, that is, our physical and social location in life. Whether we recognize it or not, too many of our lives—especially in our cities—are functionally segregated by issues of race and class.

In the midst of these color lines that define racial division, could it be that our ability to analyze or empathize is contingent on the horizons of our physical and social landscape? What might it look like for thoughtful Christians to engage in meaningful reflection about race in the cities and neighborhoods that we share? As we wrestle with why color lines continue to hold such power in our society, we must understand how race is a complex, embodied reality that is always shaped by its cultural and geographic context.

What might it look like for thoughtful Christians to engage in meaningful reflection about race in the cities and neighborhoods that we share?

Race Remixed

It was 1992. The fires from the Los Angeles riots were still smoldering, but I was in class in what felt like a distant land: the Pacific Northwest.

"Do you eat a lot of rice?"

I can't remember exactly why my teacher in a required eighth-grade course on Washington state history asked me this question in front of the entire class, but I do recall the embarrassment of being put on the spot about what kind of food my mom cooked at home. I think we were covering the 1882 Chinese Exclusion Act, and somehow the conversation shifted to me, the only Asian person in the room who happened to be Chinese and therefore the authority on what all Chinese people eat.

“Uh . . . yeah, I guess,” I somewhat awkwardly replied. Truthfully, I was certain we ate amounts of rice that would be considered “a lot” in the eyes of my peers, but I also knew that too much certainty in my reply would only cement the stereotype. At the time, I couldn’t have explained why the question made me want to slump down in my chair and disappear, but it was hardly the first or last type of comment I would receive about being Chinese.

Does anyone really enjoy junior high school? As if the awkwardness of puberty isn’t enough to deal with, the social environment of adolescence can be challenging to say the least. It seems that nearly anything and everything can be used to create cliques and hierarchies, or to establish social dominance of some kind. Height, hair, athletic ability, shoes, attractiveness (or in other words: race, class, and gender), and that elusive “cool” factor everyone craves, can make or break the fragile identities being constructed in adolescence.

My first memories of racial consciousness (though I certainly wouldn’t have called it that at the time) were the simple by-product of wanting to fit in with everyone else, like most teenagers. Though I wasn’t incessantly teased or bullied, the regular playground taunts and classroom slights that are virtually universal to the Asian American experience certainly created a distinct feeling of otherness and isolation that accompanied my apparently Chinese body. It didn’t matter that there were over a billion Chinese people in the world; in these places, I was too often a “perpetual foreigner”[2] with an uncanny ability to speak unaccented English.

The one place where my alleged otherness seemed irrelevant was church—a suburban, Chinese American, evangelical church. Here my appearance and cultural experiences blended in with everyone else, and we could all take a deep, relaxing breath of racial familiarity. Here my social identity was formed and nurtured, even if I didn't realize it was happening. Looking back, any explicit conversation about race was curiously absent from our church—perhaps because being Asian American was simply assumed to be normal, just like being white was the cultural norm at my public school.

But just because we didn't talk about race didn't make it any less real or important in our lives. In hindsight, it's clear that a form of racial rationale—the social logic of homogeneity, if you will—was foundational to our existence as a group. It was comfortable, assumed, and it was *us*. The identifying categories were on the church sign out front and in the "ethnic" faces of everyone in the congregation. Though we never named the rationale, we all knew how it worked, perhaps making the conversation unnecessary. Or so we thought.

It seems to me that there's a similarly absent conversation missing from much of the evangelical church today, a church that still largely falls along color lines and adopts the same racial logic of grouping into "sames."[3] Though there's certainly been slow and steady progress in broaching the race conversation in some churches and Christian circles (depending on geography and social location), not a whole lot has changed about the racial assumptions and divisions we accept as normal, even if many of us have learned to adjust our vocabulary and speak more carefully on the topic.

Is there anything more contentious than talking about race?

Is there anything more contentious than talking about race? Though racial discourse in society marches on (too often in polarizing media sound bites and online echo chambers), many evangelicals seem reluctant to contribute something different and constructive to the conversation. Soft tolerance, naive postracialism, unintentional tokenism, or some combination of the three is often the default posture toward issues of race among many Christians.[4] More than fifteen years after the groundbreaking book *Divided by Faith: Evangelical Religion and the Problem of Race in America*, many fundamental questions about race remain largely unexamined, and many complex challenges remain in place. Sometimes the change we seek or imagine is much slower than we realize, even when we think we understand the root problems.

However, from another perspective, and in different corners of the North American religious landscape, there have also been a lot of hopeful developments in Christian engagement with race over the last decade. As national demographics continue to diversify, and historic progress marches onward, more thoughtful evangelicals are paying attention to leaders, literature, and conferences on multiethnic churches, racial reconciliation, and contemporary issues such as immigration reform. In the midst of these developments, is there really a need for *another* book about race from a Christian perspective? I believe there is.

One of the unique dimensions of the race conversation I hope to explore in this book is the way in which the convergence of race and *place*, particularly in urban contexts, is essential for a Christian understanding of moving toward reconciliation in our communities. Rather than rehashing race from sociological, psychological, or historical perspectives (though I will certainly draw on those disciplines), I want to focus on the intersection of *theology* and *geography*. Wherever I teach and speak, I find that so many thoughtful, well-intentioned Christians want to "do something" about racial disparities, and yet as they examine their lives in an effort to act, they bump up against obstacles and limitations. It seems to me that many of those blockages are geographic in nature, determined by the limits of time and effort in the context of place and location.

My sense is that race—and theology, for that matter—looks different from where you stand, and that our horizons often depend on the particular structures, systems, and stories we encounter in our cities. Thinking Christianly about geography is simply examining *where* we're standing, and then understanding how exactly those positions and locations shape our everyday faith and practice. Perhaps exploring some of these places in our lives more intentionally will shift and stretch our horizons of truth, goodness, and beauty in what St. Augustine called the "city of God."

Mapping Our Way

In order to frame this journey conceptually, the following road map should provide a rough sketch of where we're going. Part one of the book, "Race and Place," sets the stage by unpacking some terms and ideas that will be used throughout the book such as race, place, and colorblindness. Through exploring intersections of theology and geography, I will use the garden-to-city narrative as a backdrop for making sense of the Christian story, and for our missional responsibility to inhabit that story more intentionally with a lived theology of place.

Part two, "Patterns of Exclusion," examines the structures of racial division in our cities and communities by identifying the color lines that shape our lives through segregation, isolation, and walls of hostility. By diagnosing the challenges we face as structural, geographic, and spiritual, I will look at historic and contemporary urban issues such as housing, education, and gentrification in order to propose a way forward from hostility to community.

Finally, part three, "Communities of Belonging," focuses on crossing color lines by presenting a practical theology of reconciliation through the lens of family, communion, and neighborhood renewal. Through unlearning the social logic of homogeneity, I will offer some postures and practices of place that foster reflective action for pastors, ministry practitioners, activists, and everyday neighbors and community builders.

Throughout these various vignettes of theology and geography, I hope to map a distinctly Christian vision of racial reconciliation that challenges the church to dig deeper into the soil that structures our lives together. Only by transgressing the socially constructed lines of racial division can we begin to reimagine places that cultivate human flourishing instead of strife. If I am right in assuming that geography indeed determines much of our perspective on race, then the purpose of this book is to provide some tools to (1) better understand the "placed" contexts of our racial division and (2) practice ways of being a new kind of community that reshapes our cities and neighborhoods in the image of divine belonging. Simply put, we must be Christian in all the places we've located our lives, and we must do it together.

To assume something as challenging and complex as racial division will just work itself out without serious reflection and radical praxis is dangerously naive, and for many, even life threatening. The status quo of isolation and segregation has been too costly, and too many vulnerable and valuable lives in places of exclusion have been lost along the way. Sadly, so many of the signs on our streets point to abuses of power, cries of pain and outrage, and elusive structural inequities that "all land, with great violence, upon the body."[5] Regardless of our color or creed, we cannot ignore how much these precious lives matter in the eyes of God. So let's read the street signs a little more closely, dig deep with new determination, and link arms with our neighbors in solidarity and love. I hope we'll find the courage, conviction, and creativity to follow the Spirit into uncharted territory.

Simply put, we must be Christian in all the places we've located our lives, and we must do it together.

PART I

RACE & PLACE

Beginning the Journey

\- 1 -

Theology and Geography

In elementary school one of my social studies assignments was to memorize the fifty states and their capitals, a geographic task that still eludes me today. Even by the time I got to college, I cannot say that I understood geography to be about much more than naming the many different places on maps. Perhaps for you the term *geography* simply elicits the same images—a globe with many labels, or detailed maps with pins and boundaries. Well, it turns out that the field of geography is in fact much more than maps, and while *physical* geography is indeed concerned with topography, cartography, and the like, it is *human* and *cultural* geography that will be a point of focus in this book.

Human and cultural geographies explore how people and communities understand their environments, particularly in terms of space and place. Even more specifically, *urban* geography often focuses on the built environment of cities, and the ways in which people make sense of the places where they live, work, and play. The reality that we construct meaning from our geography is both practical and theological. Not only is it impossible to abstract our lives from our physical environment, but it is also an essential theological truism that context—linguistic, cultural, geographic, and otherwise—powerfully shapes our Christian faith and practice, and always has.

Jesus *of Nazareth* was a first-century recognition that Jesus came from, and was shaped by, a particular place and the local communities found there. The Sea of Galilee, the region of Samaria, the road to Jericho, the city of Jerusalem, and the hillsides, homes, and synagogues therein were specific geographies that defined Jesus' life and ministry.

Stand in the Place Where You Live

Think about the sorts of places that have shaped your life. The 1989 R.E.M. song "Stand" suggests that we think about place: "Stand in the place where you live. . . . Think about direction, wonder why you haven't before."[1] How often do you think about the place where you live? In between the hours of commuting, screen time, and the busy routines of the rat race, do we ever pause to really pay attention to the geography around us? And by "pay attention," I mean linger and contemplate longer than it takes for the traffic light to change. But who has time for that?

Long before I began my formal studies in theology, I was inhabiting spaces and places that shaped my faith. Often this shaping was subtle and unintentional, or so it seemed. Sanctuaries and shopping malls were like the geographic wallpaper of my life: noticeable, and at times decorative, but not all that important in the grand scheme of things. However, as I've come to understand my own story and the forces that have shaped my Christian identity, it's become impossible for me to ignore the structures and textures of the variety of places that have made me who I am. In the same way that a liquid fills the shape of its container, places—specifically urban places—have shaped my life like a mold.

Place, simply put for now, is how humans make sense of geography or location. It's the meaning and memory we attach to spaces we inhabit, the physical context of our lives. Place is the sense of home we feel in a familiar house, or on a certain street. It's the idea of holy ground or sacred land—the suggestion that dirt or concrete might be more than the sum of its parts. We ought to truly pay attention to the places in our lives, specifically the places that make cities what they are. For many years, my friend Ray Bakke has been saying that the Christian story "begins in a garden and ends in a city,"[2] and part of the assumption behind that observation is that gardens and cities are not simply spaces for plants and streets. Rather, they are the essential and specific environments in which we begin to make sense of our world—the world that God has created and redeemed, and intends to restore.

> ***Place*** **is how humans make sense of geography or location. It's the meaning and memory we attach to spaces we inhabit, the physical context of our lives.**

Just Down the Street

Over the years, I've lived on a lot of different streets. From the time I was born in Ann Arbor, Michigan, to the year I started college at the University of Washington in Seattle, I had moved over ten times, amassing a large collection of home addresses along the way. Many of the streets I can vaguely recall, but my most vivid childhood memories return to Lindley Drive in suburban Raleigh, North Carolina.

Lindley Drive was a quiet, tree-lined residential street that ended in a classic suburban cul-de-sac that served as the default recreation area for all the neighborhood kids. Packs of us would run, ride, and play up and down the block until the sun went down. All the families knew each other, and we were in and out of different neighbors' homes all the time. I'm not sure how my parents always knew where my sisters and I were at any given time, but we always managed to find our way back home. Throughout the barbecues, summer sweet tea, and long games of hide-and-seek, many tastes of Southern hospitality are etched in my memory. It never occurred to me that we were the only Asian family on our street (and probably in the entire neighborhood), and aside from the occasional curiosity about what was being served for dinner, I hadn't a clue what it meant to be "Asian," let alone third-generation Chinese American. In that sense, ignorance was bliss.

Lindley Drive as I remember it stands in stark contrast to some very different streets in Detroit that I drove down in the winter of 2010, the year my grandfather passed away. Before World War II, my grandparents emigrated from southern China to Detroit, where they worked for decades in the city running a Chinese laundry. But over time as the city changed, like most folks who weren't African American they moved to the outer suburbs, fleeing the predominantly black neighborhoods that made up most of the city. As the funeral procession drove south into Detroit toward Forest Lawn Cemetery, we crossed the outer roads, each one named by its mile marker from the downtown area. 12 Mile Road, 11 Mile Road, 10 . . . and as we crossed the infamous 8 Mile Road, the historical racial boundary between the city of Detroit and its northern suburbs, the streets started to change in dramatic fashion.

Block by block, storefronts became more dilapidated, corners more abandoned, except for the occasional liquor store or minimart, and the general feeling of decay was displayed in a drab palette of gray concrete and cracked asphalt. Some blocks felt nearly apocalyptic, with burned-out properties that seemed long deserted. For me, the fact that we were mourning the death of my grandfather was framed by another kind of sadness—the apparent loss and decline of communities that once thrived. Though urban Detroit is not without signs of life and rejuvenation today, much of the city is still marred by years of neglect and questions about the future. I often wonder when the streets of Detroit will flourish again. What would it take to see hope restored in a place like Detroit, where multiple members of my family first put down their roots in pursuit of the American dream?

Questions that arise from the streets where we live, work, and play are not only for the residents of those particular places. Rather, it's important to remember how the urban geographies that frame much of our lives—the places we sleep, garden, worship, and greet neighbors—are not simply incidental to our schedules and priorities. In fact, the very fabric of our most deeply held beliefs and values, including our cultural identities themselves, are intimately shaped by cul-de-sacs and grocery stores, parking lots and freeway overpasses, and the lives of others we encounter there.

What can we learn about our communities and ourselves as we examine the disparities between the Lindley Drives and 8 Mile Roads of our increasingly urbanized world? Urban scholar John Rennie Short puts it succinctly in *The Urban Order*: "Cities . . . are a mirror of our societies, a part of our economy, an element of our environments. But above all else they are a measure of our ability to live with each other. When we examine our cities, we examine ourselves."[3] I agree that some self-examination is in order.

Walls and bridges didn't build themselves, and neither did Walmart or public housing just show up overnight. How should we feel about the urban environment we've built for ourselves? These fixtures of our cities are reflections of us and our collective understanding (or misunderstanding) of life together. Streets are much more than concrete and asphalt—they are physical manifestations of the lifeblood of our neighborhoods. They are signs, both pragmatic and instructive, as well as deeply symbolic and meaningful. On the surface, street signs identify and direct, but in a broader sense, street signs are all around us. How might we begin to read these signs more deeply in order to glean all they have to say to us?

Signs of the Times

"And now the end has come. So listen to my piece of advice: exegesis, exegesis, and yet more exegesis! Keep to the Word, to the Scripture that has been given to us."[4] These parting words of Karl Barth to his German students in 1935 reflect the absolute importance of reading Scripture closely, and the centrality of critical interpretation in understanding the Bible rightly. For as long as I can remember, my evangelical upbringing instilled in me a deep passion for God's Word and a desire to study the discipline of exegesis.

Although seminary prepared me with skills for thoughtful biblical exegesis, the importance of "cultural exegesis," of reading and interpreting *cultural* texts, seemed secondary. Theologian Kevin Vanhoozer addresses this very matter, saying that "Christians must learn to read the signs of the times. . . . Most of us learn to read and write. . . . What we do not learn, however, is *cultural literacy*: how to 'read' and 'write' *culture*."[5]

Much like the term *place*, the word *culture* is difficult to define succinctly, but for now, the aspect of cultural literacy I want to focus on is reading the built environment of the city. In other words, how do physical locations, and the *places* we create in those locations, communicate meaning beyond the structures themselves? This question is just as important as the biblical inquiries we wrestle with in our close readings of Scripture because we simply cannot escape or

How do physical locations, and the *places* we create in those locations, communicate meaning beyond the structures themselves?

untangle ourselves from the physical contexts in which we read the Bible. It has always been this way and will continue to be a challenge as long as faithful Bible readers continue to affirm the complex divine-and-human nature through which God reveals himself in the world.

A deep reading of both the Scriptures and the city is essential to understanding the signs of the times. This is as true in the streets of Ferguson, Missouri, where Michael Brown's lifeless body laid for hours before riots engulfed the community, as it is in the streets of Urumqi, Xinjiang, where persecuted ethnic minority Uighurs have frequently clashed with Chinese police officers. In the midst of these urban realities, questions of race, place, and reconciliation must be on the hearts and minds of faithful Christians.

Bringing theology and geography into conversation is not purely an academic exercise. More precisely, it is an attempt to step back from the Christian beliefs we hold in order to see them more fully in the environments that shape them. Only by doing so can we practice Christianity faithfully, especially given that Christianity has never been simply a doctrine or set of ideas to affirm in our hearts and minds. Rather, as Orthodox theologian Georges Florovsky reminds us,

> Christianity entered history as a new social order, or rather a new social dimension. From the very beginning Christianity was not primarily a "doctrine," but exactly a "community." There was not only a "Message" to be proclaimed and delivered, and "Good News" to be declared. There was precisely a New Community, distinct and peculiar, in the process of growth and formation, to which members were called and recruited. Indeed, "fellowship" was the basic category of Christian existence.[6]

This new community, this peculiar fellowship of people who radically reshaped the social world around them, was deeply embedded in the cultures, lands, and communities of their local geographies. Even as they affirmed their heavenly citizenship (Phil 3:20), they did so as dual citizens in the Roman world. On the street corners of Roman colonies and in the tenements of port cities on the Mediterranean, early Christians lived out their faith wherever God placed them.

The Scriptures they revered, the prayers they prayed, and the meals they shared were intimately connected to the textures of place that framed their lives. Perhaps the most surprising and beautiful outcome of these early Christian communities was the unusual character of their social lives, which defied cultural norms of separation by race, class, and gender. Somehow the early Christians understood and actually practiced a gospel that reconciled people across both color lines and the innumerable lines of land, language, and religion. Their fellowship was a symbol and enactment of the kingdom of God, a sign that the time was ripe for God's reign to create something new in the world. They believed that in Christ there was "neither Jew nor Gentile, neither slave nor free, nor is there male and female" (Gal 3:28). What did these Christians understand about following Jesus that created such radical communities of belonging?

Early Christian Community and Belonging

Before I move too quickly toward romanticizing early Christian communities, it's important to recognize that the radical nature of the social character of the early church did not come easily or overnight. Though the first followers of the Way inhabited relatively cosmopolitan places like Philippi, Ephesus, and Corinth, getting Jews and Gentiles together was not high on the social agenda of the church, as if some strategy for diversity would further their cause. In other words, the ethnic mixing we see among early Christians was not the result of some ancient affirmative action program, or an intentional outreach to cultural others to give the appearance of equal opportunity. First-century Jews, like most ethnic groups of the time, were very ethnocentric and tended to self-segregate.

So what happened? How could God's chosen people, commanded to be holy and separate from the "unclean" Gentiles, change their fundamental understanding of community, identity, and everyday social practices? Well, it began with an evolution in how they understood God. This gradual change occurred as they saw God at work in the person of Jesus, and then witnessed the subsequent fruit of the Holy Spirit.

Long before Jesus showed up on the scene, the people of Israel understood that Yahweh was one. "Hear, O Israel: The LORD our God, the LORD is one" (Deut 6:4). This liturgical refrain echoed in the hearts and minds of faithful Israelites whenever they gathered for worship. The uniqueness of Israel's monotheism relative to their pagan neighbors is well documented, but there are two scandals on which to focus: the scandal of ethnic particularity and the scandal of the incarnation.

The first scandal is essentially the doctrine of election, or the chosenness of Israel over against all others to be *the* people to redeem *all* peoples. Among all the various tribes and peoples of the ancient Near Eastern world, God chose Israel, and accordingly did *not* choose the Edomites, the Philistines, the Assyrians, or anyone else. Yahweh continually reminded God's people that "the LORD your God has chosen you out of all the peoples on the face of the earth to be his people, his treasured possession" (Deut 7:6). Naturally, the unique idea that there is only one true God in the cosmos—that the "gods" of other peoples are therefore false, and that the one true God has chosen you for a special task—tends to breed some ethnocentrism.

Enter Jesus of Nazareth. Jesus arrived as the fulfillment of Israel's story, but not at all in the way people expected. It didn't take long for his followers to recognize that Jesus had a special relationship with Yahweh, and that this intimate familial relationship was unlike that of other rabbis, prophets, or would-be messiahs. Even though it took quite some time for the disciples to grasp the full meaning of Jesus as fully God *and* human, as Jesus went to the cross and emerged on the other side of death his divine nature became more salient. Could Jesus truly be God in the flesh? And more paradoxically, could God become human? The incarnation is an absolute scandal, but for the moment let's try to wrestle with the frankly strange notion that God could have a body.

If God has a human body, and that body is fleshed out in Jesus of Nazareth, then somehow in the almighty and eternal God of the universe we find all the particularity of a first-century, thirty-something, Aramaic-speaking, male Jewish rabbi from a small town in Galilee during a time of political unrest. Like all people, Jesus got hungry, he experienced real emotions, his sandals got dusty and sweaty, and he even experienced indigestion on occasion just like the rest of us humans. God's body matters for many reasons, but try pausing to consider the ordinary, fleshly, material, and finite nature of Jesus' humanity that somehow coexists with the transcendent, immaterial, infinite Creator God of the cosmos. Simply put, the incarnation signals to us not only God's great love for creation, but also the sanctity and importance of the body, and its particular ethnicity, language, culture, and place.

In Jesus, the early Christians encountered the face of God, and when Jesus transgressed the boundaries of race, class, and gender, as he was often prone to do, the disciples were seeing God's hands at work in reshaping the divided world they knew.

But the more they saw God in Jesus—and Jesus in God—the more they were entering into another scandalous notion: God is not one. Or more precisely, God is not *only* one.

By the time the Holy Spirit showed up at Pentecost, and the authority of the Father and Jesus was granted to the disciples via the ministry and gifting of the Spirit, the divine family portrait was complete, even if more official notions of the "Trinity" would take centuries to formalize. God is three and God is one; God is community. In the language of the creeds, the persons of the Trinity are "coequal and coeternal," but more importantly for our purposes, God can *only* be God in community, and the divine community perfectly models unity in diversity, mutuality, and belonging.

These are weighty theological ideas we'll unpack more throughout the book, but let's return briefly to those early ethnocentric Christians one more time. There they were, minding their own business, wrestling with what Judaism would look like now that Jesus had risen. This was no small task. But as they were doing their thing—keeping the sabbath, observing food laws, and embracing all the cultural markers of God's people—suddenly, something strange started happening.

This communal God, through the power and ministry of the Holy Spirit, started showing up in formerly desolate and forbidden places—the lives of the very people who were others, outsiders, and unclean. As we read in the book of Acts, God was pouring out his Spirit, again and again, on people who really had no business encountering the God of Israel in such powerful and intimate ways. These strangers were uncircumcised, pork-eating, sabbath-breaking Gentiles. They didn't walk, talk, or look the part to God-fearing Jews, but somehow they had received the same Spirit the apostles encountered. They were foreigners and pagans, but God was somehow making them into a new family and an adoptive household. This "estrangement-turned-reconciliation" is the heart of God whose very nature is radical belonging in community. And it all took place in real time and space, with particular personalities, cultures, and geographies.

For these odd and eclectic communities on the edges of the Roman Empire, Christian discipleship was not "racially diverse" only because of ideology or identity politics. Rather, faithful discipleship followed the unusual direction of the Spirit, whose geographic movement seemed to cross every border. As Christians gathered around the table for fellowship—rich and poor, Jew and Greek, male and female, slave and free—they joined with one another in ways the world had not yet seen and could not understand. The only explanation, for some, was that God was finally making the world right and that God's kingdom was arriving by healing the divisions of a broken world. Even if the route and the terrain were often rocky and unpredictable, the signs of God's reconciling reign were spreading throughout Jerusalem, Judea, Samaria, and beyond.

Faithful discipleship followed the unusual direction of the Spirit, whose geographic movement seemed to cross every border.

Location, Location, Location

But what does all of this mean for us in the here and now, seemingly so far removed from those places long ago? My wife has been a licensed real estate agent for over a decade, and over the years we've learned a lot about the economics of place, which are motivated by much more than just dollars and cents. While the amounts of capital at stake are significant, and the pressures to make a good investment are powerful, the most desirable locations are not simply assessed by their price tag. The "location, location, location" mantra follows patterns of both social and economic capital; we desire places that affirm both our identities and our bank accounts. Where and how we live reflects something about us, or at least how we tend to see and understand ourselves.

For nearly that same decade, our family has lived one block off Martin Luther King Jr. Way South in Seattle's Rainier Valley, a historically diverse, vibrant, and yet often underresourced community. It's probably not surprising to know that in every city where a street, boulevard, or avenue is named after Dr. King, you will likely find some common "urban" characteristics.[7] Is it simply coincidence that in cities across the country, poor communities of color have clustered around streets named after MLK? We anticipate certain types of people and places in the neighborhoods along MLK, and this is signified by the street name. For the most part, we have loved living near MLK for all these years, but we recognize that much of the perception of desirability has to do with an intangible sense of belonging. We all want to locate ourselves in a place that feels like "us."

Where exactly do you belong? What kind of places do you most identify with? Whatever belonging is, it involves belonging *with* and *to* others in a place. This is how communities work: people and places help us to know who we are. It's fundamentally human to desire belonging, to pursue commonality, to want to know others and be known; this is how we make sense of our identities. And as we've noted, this desire to belong is also the stamp of the Creator, in whose image we are made for community.

But could it also be true that our desire for belonging can become distorted by fear, pride, or self-deception? Is it possible that our longing to be safe, known, or comfortable could lead us to places of isolation and even idolatry? It's clear to me that we tend to locate our lives—in ways that go beyond our home address—around the same social logic that kept Israel looking inward for so many generations. Perhaps it's the same racial rationale that drives real estate: that we belong to and with each other as long as we are the same. When we share the same educational background, ethnic identity, cultural values, and political views, then yes, of course, we think we are experiencing "belonging"!

But this is precisely the opposite definition of belonging from what we see in the community of God that spills over from the Father, Son, and Spirit into the world. It is not that belonging and sameness are mutually exclusive; we can and should experience healthy forms of cultural familiarity and shared values that nurture our identities in important ways. However, when we *only* or even *primarily* experience belonging in homogeneity—racial, cultural, religious, or otherwise—then I believe we are tragically missing out and falling short of the deeply transformative divine community that must accompany authentic Christian discipleship. Simply put, life in Christ should have a profound effect on the shape of our desire for belonging and the character of Christ's body in the world.

If we cannot model this Christian belonging in the world of real estate, then perhaps we do not actually understand what it means to be Christian. In his remarkable book *The Christian Imagination: Theology and the Origins of Race,* Dr. Willie Jennings offers a challenge along these lines:

> The identities being formed in the space of communion may become a direct challenge to the geographic patterns forced upon peoples by the capitalistic logic of real estate. We who live in the new space of joining may need to transgress the boundaries of real estate, by buying where we should not and living where we must not, by living together where we supposedly cannot, and being identified with those whom

> we should not. . . . For us in the racial world, the remade world, a crucial point of discipleship is precisely global real estate. . . . The story of race is also the story of place.[8]

Jennings suggests that the "logic" of real estate in our profit-driven world depends on patterns of racial homogeneity and cultural sameness that perpetuate injustices of hierarchy and separation. Markets function efficiently with a "divide and conquer" rationale. But Christian identities are formed by *joining*—with God, with neighbors, with land—and the space in which this occurs closely resembles the most profound joining, that of Jesus' life and death with our own. Christians belong to God, and when we locate our lives inside God's communal life, we find that we truly belong to one another in ways that transgress and transcend the world's ways of belonging.

How can I cultivate a desire for divine belonging in my own life, especially when the logic of real estate and the geography of race are so deeply embedded in my surroundings? Strangely enough, perhaps it begins with a community that simply inhabits the fullness of the Christian story, but before we go down that road, it will be important to explore the particularly difficult task of tackling the topic of race, especially in the evangelical church.

\- 2 -

Colorblind?

"But David, I don't see you as Chinese or Asian American—I just see you as a person. Why do you keep bringing up race? We're all just people—the human race, right?"

I've heard varieties of this sentiment for years, in and outside the classroom, the church, and the neighborhood. On one level, I can sympathize with the good intentions behind this suggestion. I agree that there's only one human race, and at the end of the day, people are just people, and there is much we have in common.

However, this notion of colorblindness—that we shouldn't see color, or that race doesn't matter—is also dangerously naive. It's *naive* because extensive social science and psychological research has shown, time and time again, that we humans are intricately entangled with many *unconscious biases* that shape our perception of others, our fears and assumptions, and our social behavior.[1] Try as we may, these hidden prejudices consistently surface in our words, actions, and attitudes toward others, no matter how nice or openminded we think we are. To be fair, we certainly have some level of control over how we choose to act or speak in the face of racial stereotypes, but to deny that they are an active part of our world or to suggest we can simply ignore these biases is silly and doesn't square with the best research we have about how race works.

However, presuming the merit of colorblindness is *dangerous* because it ignores the persistent lessons of history and the myriad ways that racial groups have been invented and discriminated against throughout history, often based on arbitrary physical characteristics or imagined cultural groupings. When we take an honest look at the history of race, especially in the United States, William Faulkner reminds us that "the past is never dead. It's not even past."[2] Even as laws and demographics change, the ugly history of racial conflict has left deep scars on our cultural landscape, whose many wounds continue to resurface. Colorblindness hastily glosses over these scars that have become structural realities and instead imagines a premature arrival to the land of equal opportunity and pure meritocracy.

But what does this alleged colorblindness have to do with place or geography? One of the most common missteps that occurs when we talk about race is the tendency to frame the conversation primarily as individuals, or more specifically, in the context of individualism. This tendency lifts racial issues out of their vital context—the structures of society, many of which are geographic in nature—and reduces the conversation to one about individual morality, or personal responsibility. The logic goes something like this: if we all just tried a little harder to be nice, colorblind individuals, and we stopped talking about race so much, then racism and its ill effects on our society would fade away into the fairness and equality we all proclaim as right and good. Similarly, the Christian version of this thinking bears some resemblance: if each individual Christian would just pray a little harder and read the Bible with more sincerity, then racial division would gradually recede as we worship Jesus together.

Unfortunately, as much as I wish this were possible, there are two related flaws in this logic. First, it does not take into account the complex nature of how groups (especially racial groups) and systems function in our society and in the church to shape identity. Second, it does not make space for the structural nature of social/political power and its many effects on how communities establish norms, boundaries, and authority. Simply put, when we think about race primarily as an issue of individual morality or responsibility, we lose the forest for the trees and neglect the critical issues of scale that always shape the bigger picture of race relations in society.

Whenever I facilitate conversations about race, I notice that many of our initial impulses are to identify ourselves as "good people." As we react to the shameful connotations of racism, it seems that we reflexively want to defend ourselves with "I'm not a racist!" and "I'm not a judgmental person!" This impulse, while understandable, is somewhat missing the point. Rarely do I encounter a student or churchgoer who harbors an active, explicit prejudice against another racial group. But as I often say in my classroom, if this lack of overt racism means that I'm not a racist and you're not a racist, then why is there still so much racial inequality and conflict today? Surely, there must be some explanation for this disconnection.

What place and geography do, at least in part, is provide a window into the systems and structures of race so that we can see more clearly how racial issues such as segregation are not simply the result of "bad apples," or individual people with mean prejudices. Rather, the challenges of race that plague our cities are often rooted in how groups seek and maintain power (either implicitly or explicitly), how cultural patterns become physical structures, and how impersonal systems grow to protect the interests of those in power over time. In other words, geography reveals how race works systemically and not just individually.

Geography reveals how race works systemically and not just individually.

Identity, Society, and Belonging

One autumn afternoon, when my oldest son, Jonas, was just two and a half years old, we pulled into the parking lot of the Seattle Supermarket, an ethnic grocery store a few blocks up the hill from our home. Our neighborhood has historically been home to many Asian immigrants, and the Seattle Supermarket stocks an eclectic mix of produce and groceries common to Chinese, Vietnamese, Filipino, and other Asian communities. In addition to my fifteen years of shopping there, Jonas had been regularly coming along for all of his young life.

Though my wife, Chris, and I had anticipated nothing more than a routine grocery stop, that day was different. For some reason, Jonas refused to get out of his car seat and kept making the grumpy facial expressions that displeased toddlers tend to make. After repeated questions as to why he was so determined to avoid today's usual errand, he finally relented and offered a simple explanation.

"I don't like this place," he firmly stated in his little toddler voice. Genuinely puzzled, we asked why. Jonas continued, matter-of-factly, "I don't like Chinese people."

Struck by a mixture of surprise and confusion, Chris and I looked at each other with nervous smiles. "But Jonas," we said together, "*you're* Chinese." We somewhat chuckled at what seemed so obvious to us.

"No, I'm not," he confidently replied. "I'm *white*." At this point, our nervous laughter and confused expressions turned a different direction. I can't recall the immediate details of what occurred in the moment, though I suspect we simply pried him out of the car seat and went inside. But I do remember the long conversation we had afterward on the way home and into the evening. How did our sweet, innocent toddler arrive at this strange and confusing racial conclusion?

For the first couple of years of his life, we very intentionally exposed Jonas to all the people in our lives, from the many Asian faces of our family and friends to the black, white, brown, and everything in between of our church and so-called "neighborhood of nations," where more than sixty languages are spoken in one zip code. Despite what seemed to us to be a comfortable and colorful upbringing, we pondered new questions in the wake of Jonas's racial confusion.

First, what did being Chinese really mean to Jonas? Besides the signage, sounds, and smells, why did he know that the Seattle Supermarket was full of Chinese people that he disliked? What was so different about "those people" that seemed undesirable? Second, what did it mean to think he was white? Where did he even get that language, and how did he identify with it?

Our only explanation, along with the admission that he must have picked up on some conversations in our home, is that a few weeks prior to what we now call the "Seattle Supermarket incident," we had enrolled Jonas in a local preschool cooperative where he happened to be the only child of color in a class of about fifteen. We knew this wasn't ideal, but much to our surprise at the time, we had been unable to find a racially diverse preschool in our neighborhood that matched the diversity of the community. *Besides,* we presumptively thought to ourselves, *He's only two and a half! Does the lack of preschool diversity really matter at a young age?* Apparently, it did for him.

As Chris and I have continued to reflect on Jonas's racial identity formation, there are additional factors to take into consideration—his particular personality and social disposition, the powerful effects of his first social environment among peers, and so forth. But what's clear to us now is that he was being shaped, even as a toddler-turning-preschooler, by the social logic of homogeneity and the constructions of race. He knew the

Seattle Supermarket shoppers were different from his preschool friends, and he also knew that he wanted to belong to those with whom he most closely identified. Despite our insistence from birth that he was Chinese *and* American (something we have continually repeated in the years since), his rejection of a Chinese identity came, at least in part, in response to the implicit whiteness he experienced in school.

This process of understanding who we are in the face of racial categories begins early in life and is an established field of research for those who study identity development.[3] But the purpose of this story is to examine the complexity of race in one particular social context. Who is to blame for Jonas's racial confusion? Was it the prejudice of an individual who told Jonas that being Chinese was bad and being white was good? Was it personal bigotry that told Jonas he should avoid the Seattle Supermarket because of its seemingly foreign grocery shoppers? Though individuals can and do shape our perceptions of race, I hope we recognize that the collective experiences of people and the cultural systems that shape those experiences—grocery stores, classrooms, sidewalks, and playgrounds—are perhaps more explanatory and formative as a whole than isolated incidents of blatant racial prejudice. Racial logic is in the air we breathe, and racial categories are woven into the social fabric and geography of our communities.

Ignoring these social realities, or simply writing off Jonas's preoccupation with race as an extension of his parents' angst, doesn't change the fact that questions of identity are powerfully shaped by a desire for belonging and that belonging works itself out in bounded groups that live in real time and space. Local neighborhoods and the communities of people who live there provide a physical, geographic context that shapes the logic, appearance, and social outcomes of belonging.

Progressive Colorblindness

Even in a diverse neighborhood like ours where individuals repeatedly insist that they love the cultural diversity of our community, the deeper reality of belonging across color lines often falls short. For example, Chris and I used to wonder why—especially in such a culturally "progressive" place—it was so difficult to find a preschool where different kinds of kids were integrated in a diverse learning community. When people say they value diversity, why don't they work to ensure their children are educated in a culturally diverse environment? What I've come to understand, in addition to recognizing the shallow nature of superficial multiculturalism so many of our well-intentioned neighbors profess to value, is that loving diversity as individuals without accounting for the systemic nature of our neighborhood's structural inequalities is not only unhelpful. Ironically, it is also a form of colorblindness.

This colorblindness is a desire for diversity on our own terms, in ways and forms that are palatable to us as individual consumers. Rather than suggesting color doesn't matter, it is a more subtle implication that being colorful matters so long as that appearance of multiculturalism doesn't disturb the status quo of the dominant culture. Instead of being blind to racial differences altogether, it is a blindness to the systemic differences that give race its meaning in society. I sometimes call this the multicultural potluck version of diversity.

Over the years in my hood, we've held a lot of multicultural potlucks, and for the most part I'm really glad we gathered regularly to eat together because it provided many opportunities for crosscultural conversation, friendship, and the occasional recipe exchange. Multiculturalism has to start somewhere, and there's much to appreciate and celebrate in these kinds of gatherings. However, what I also came to recognize over the years was that the potlucks often tended to lack any real depth of engagement and that participants could easily walk through the buffet line, sample some culturally exotic flavors at their own discretion, sit down with a familiar face, trade some routine small talk, and then quietly return home satisfied with their taste of diversity.

Surely, this was not the only way people engaged these potlucks, and some neighbors were more intentional than I could be at forming deeper friendships, but many of us who believe we value diversity do so as individuals sampling a bit of this and a bit of that while remaining on the sidelines of a Christian reconciliation that requires much more costly personal investment. Cultural tokenism—a little taste of diversity for the sake of appearances—is not enough, and just as discipleship calls believers beyond mere church attendance, so does reconciliation demand a wider view of what's really at stake. So whether you're stuck in the first version of colorblindness ("I don't see color"), or you find yourself with a sampler plate from the table of the multicultural potluck, the root problem is the same: an inability to move from individual to systemic ways of seeing race and therefore racism as a bigger, deeper issue than our personal tastes for either sameness or difference.

Colorblindness has a kind of homogenizing effect on communities: it suggests unity through *uniformity* instead of belonging in spite of difference.

Until we're able to move beyond this shallow appreciation for diversity to the deeper questions of how and why *systems* shape the diverse life experiences of our neighbors, we'll remain on the surface of racial tensions and confused about why our colorblind and/or colorful society remains materially different for racial groups. Furthermore, both colorblindness and superficial multiculturalism in the church will perpetuate our isolation from one another as we cluster into groups of sameness. Too often, the social logic of the church has mirrored the divisions in society—whether in the name of growth or comfortable familiarity—so much so that reconciliation is seen as an extracurricular hobby for a few radical Christians, or an important issue for "those people" who live in what we perceive to be urban neighborhoods or conflict zones. Ultimately, colorblindness in all its various forms and good intentions has a kind of homogenizing effect on communities: it suggests unity through *uniformity* instead of belonging in spite of difference.

American Evangelical Individualism

But perhaps it's still unclear how race and racism are *systemic* and why this is important. Why is the systemic nature of racism so difficult to pinpoint? One of the biggest factors is the long shadow cast by American individualism and the way it frames our perspective on race.

When I first learned to write my Chinese name, my grandfather started with the family name, what most Americans would consider my surname or last name. In Chinese culture, like in many East Asian languages, the family name comes first, followed by a generational name shared with siblings, and then the unique given name is last. The individual name is last because the *group* identifiers (in this case, the family) take priority, both socially and culturally.

Not surprisingly, in much of the Western world, the opposite is true: your unique individual name comes first, hence the term "first name." In some rare instances, a last name can even become unimportant. Consider "Beyoncé"—how strange would it seem if we called her "Knowles"? Naming conventions vary widely across cultures, but they do point to larger values. Crosscultural research has long confirmed how prized rugged individualism is in American society, and some studies even indicate that the United States is the most individualistic country in the entire world![4] Whether or not the United States officially holds this title, it's clear that we Americans are a highly individualistic bunch. The autonomous, responsible, self-made, and proudly unique individual is the common denominator in our cultural landscape.

Interestingly, Emerson and Smith's *Divided by Faith* drives the point even further: "Although the larger American culture is itself highly individualistic, the close connection between faith and freewill individualism . . . renders white evangelicals even more individualistic than other white Americans."[5] When it comes to the issue of race, white evangelicals default to individualistic explanations, and this tendency is due to a toolkit that only comes with individualistic solutions. So when racial conflict arises, the thought is simply to address the *personal* sin of the perpetrator and remind them of their *personal* responsibility to treat people equally and fairly. While this certainly is a better approach than, say, outright denial of racial conflict, the limitations of a toolkit that relies so heavily on individualism are clear. How can the church be a reconciled community, let alone an agent of healing in society, if our only diagnosis is to address individual morality?

When confronted with racial conflict,

> it is a necessity for evangelicals to interpret the problem at the individual level. To do otherwise would challenge the very basis of their world, both their faith and the American way of life. . . . Suggesting social causes of the race problem challenges the cultural elements with which they construct their lives. This is the radical limitation of the white evangelical toolkit.[6]

Though Emerson and Smith do not pull any punches in their description of white evangelicals, which in fairness is not a monolithic group, the central themes of their research remain compelling, if not a little painful to acknowledge.

Emerson and Smith conclude their chapter on colorblindness with the recognition that "white evangelicals do not want a race problem. They want to see people get along, and want people to have equal opportunity. . . . In short, they yearn for colorblind people. This is the contemporary white American evangelical perspective."[7] Despite its earnest desire for harmony and fairness, this evangelical colorblindness, which should be noted is not limited to white Christians, cannot account for systemic, structural, or social causes of racism or racial inequality. And as such, we're back to where we started, where I'm not racist, you're not racist, and yet racial conflict remains whether or not we want to acknowledge it.

Immoral Society

So who is to blame for these racial issues if bad individuals are not responsible? Prominent twentieth-century theologian and ethicist Reinhold Niebuhr may help to point us in the right direction. Niebuhr's classic book *Moral Man and Immoral Society* highlights the challenge of understanding the systemic sins of society. Individuals, he suggests, have the desire and capacity to treat each other fairly and honestly. On a smaller scale, or among those with whom we share common values, we seem to be able to practice this fairness in equitable ways.

Imagine you and I are meeting for a brown-bag lunch one day, but you are in a rush and end up forgetting your food at home. I have brought some soup, and seeing that you're hungry and that I have enough for both of us, we agree to share the soup. No problem—we find another bowl and spoon, and after sharing the soup, we are both fed and satisfied.

Now let's take it a bit further. Imagine you have also brought another friend, and now there are three of us. We can probably still work something out, but there's a little less soup to go around. Not to worry—I can find something more to eat later. But what if you bring five, ten, or one hundred people with you? This starts to become much more complicated. How do I split the soup evenly? How can I arrange for the timely and equitable distribution of soup, even if I've brought a large amount? I may need some guidelines, also known as rules and policies, to ensure everyone can have some soup in the name of fairness and equal opportunity.

However, this idea of fairness is easier said than done. Even if in my heart of hearts, as an individual, I long for each person's need for soup to be equally satisfied, it is very likely that the policies I develop in my soup-sharing system will not work out for everyone. What if the soup I bring is full of wheat noodles, and you are gluten intolerant? What if the time I set to share the soup is during your work schedule? What if the line for soup sharing is long and you are not physically able to stand for an hour? What if you live too far from the soup-sharing location and no public transit is available? What if you are soup averse and favor salad instead? After fielding numerous complaints and making some adjustments, if I simply can't accommodate everyone's various needs I will likely attempt to devise an arrangement that works best for the majority of us, but regrettably excludes those with other needs.

What would inevitably occur over time is that my soup system would evolve to serve a particular group, and that group would dictate the rules of the system to serve the interests of the group. If wheat is a preferred ingredient on the menu, then I suppose I could offer sincere apologies to those who are gluten free. It's not personal, and we don't dislike you as individuals, but our system simply won't work for you.

Niebuhr suggests that here is "one of the tragedies of the human spirit: its inability to conform its collective life to its individual ideals. As individuals, men believe that they ought to love and serve each other and establish justice between each other. As racial, economic, and national groups they take for themselves, whatever their power can command."[8] It may seem like a stretch to imagine that soup sharing could become motivated by power, but consider the unspoken power dynamics of most soup kitchens that serve people who are unsheltered or chronically homeless. Do people attend mandatory chapel services before meals solely out of spiritual devotion? Nearly every inner-city rescue mission with a feeding program that I know of operates with altruistic, Christian ideals of love of neighbor at the heart of what they do. Yet because of the systemic complexities of groups in society (identity, power, etc.), there is always a struggle to practice and realize these ideals that so many individuals uphold as important.

The social ills we face will not likely go away without significant efforts to reform *both* our individual ethics and the systems we live in.

In this sense, race and racism are quite similar to poverty and hunger, since many of the challenges are systemic in nature. As individuals, and especially in the church, we want to treat people justly with love, kindness, and equity. But as a society, we often fall short of those ideals as we get into the daily process of actually working it out. This obviously doesn't preclude the possibility of making meaningful progress in feeding people, caring for those in need, or practicing reconciliation, but Niebuhr reminds us that the good intentions of individuals often bump up against the imperfect systemic realities of society, and no matter how hard we try to be personally moral, responsible, and Christian, the social ills we face will not likely go away without significant efforts to reform *both* our individual ethics and the systems we live in that inherently function with bias and prejudice.

Race, Place, and Discipleship

So far in this chapter, we've spent a lot of time describing and diagnosing a problem: the acute limitations of seeing race solely as an issue of individual morality. But how does geography help us to move in a new direction to see the bigger picture that seems so complex and at times overwhelming? Here let's consider the call of Christian discipleship as it relates to colorblindness.

If there's one thing I've learned over the years from my friend and colleague Brian Bantum, it's the idea that race is like a type of discipleship. More precisely, the logic of race is a kind of formation, a type of twisted "discipleship" into *deformation*, where race shapes us into its rationale and ways of being. Race does enormous formative work in our world. It is not enough to suggest that racism is only individual fear, prejudice, or ignorance. When we examine the history and scope of race, and its powerful ability to shape society, we have to acknowledge the pivotal role that racial logic plays in the development and deployment of colonialism, capitalism, and modernity itself.[9] This is of course an enormous argument, but regardless of how we see the severity of this situation, we must recognize that the Christian faith was never a passive observer in these developments. It's not as if Christianity just happened to innocently coincide with the emergence of the modern world without being shaped by that world.

Rather, the rise of Christianity in the modern era, like all religious movements, revealed a culturally embedded faith whose language, ideas, and practices were inevitably entangled with the worldviews and social norms of the day. Christianity grew up inside a world whose racial logic defines and defends biological hierarchies, slavery as a matter of course, and "racial purity" as morally good. While these arrangements were hardly the sole responsibility of Christianity, what I want to emphasize is Christianity's complicity and entanglement with the deep architecture of these cultural norms, even as more prophetic voices in this same Christianity ran counter to these assumptions.

One way to frame this central dysfunction is what Dr. Willie Jennings has simply called "racial faith," a kind of Christian faith that is tainted with and intimately shaped by racial sensibilities. The result, which persists today in various forms, is that "Christianity in the Western world lives and moves within a diseased social imagination."[10] In the context of discipleship, particularly in the racialized United States, Jennings repeatedly asks: "Why does racial faith seem so much more decisive than Christian faith?" In other words, why does Christian belonging so predictably fall along color lines when we say the gospel reconciles *all* people to God and to one another? It's apparent that we have some real work to do when it comes to Christian discipleship—a discipleship that is tainted with both the distortions of racial logic and the mistaken notions of colorblindness.

As we noted in the first chapter, discipleship never occurs in some abstract space apart from the places that we inhabit to make sense of our lives. We don't live above the land or independent of geography and its influence on us. Even the most basic notion of discipleship—that of *following* Jesus—has geographic connotations. How do we understand Jesus' location, and where do we see Jesus coming from and going to? Exactly where is the Spirit at work in our world? To be good followers, we must have a decent sense of direction, a good lay of the land, as well as attentive hearts, minds, and feet when it comes to getting in step with Jesus. Last, but perhaps most importantly, we must also be prepared to follow the triune God into some unfamiliar places.

Going Through Samaria

Every day, mostly without thinking, we transition from place to place and adhere to the social norms where we find ourselves. Weather permitting, we may relax on a lunch break outside, while we more carefully watch our language and posture in an important meeting. When we travel, near or far, we largely adopt the "when in Rome" mentality of cultural adaptation. Some refer to these phenomena as code-switching or social scripts, and Jesus was no exception to these ways of managing human interactions while paying attention to the local environment.

However, Jesus was also known to repeatedly push the boundaries of these social norms as he went, often boldly, into places where he didn't belong. At times, Jesus seems to utterly toss aside the cultural rules of engagement that so precisely circumscribed Jewish life in the first century. Nowhere is this clearer than in Jesus' well-known and controversial conversation with a Samaritan woman at a well (Jn 4). What can we glean about race, place, and discipleship from this familiar text?

Two concise but essential verses provide some geographic orientation in the setup to this passage:

> So he left Judea and went back once more to Galilee. Now he had to go through Samaria. (Jn 4:3-4)

As Jesus' reputation is growing throughout the region, he decides to travel with his disciples from Judea, in the south near Jerusalem, back home to Nazareth in Galilee. But right smack in the middle of this journey is Samaria, an entire region that many Jews would intentionally avoid because of their long-standing ethnic conflict with Samaritans, who they viewed as racially impure and religiously compromised due to their inter-marriage with cultural others. The common practice of Jews walking all the way *around* Samaria was a small price to pay in the name of keeping with the social norms that dictated separation and purity.

But these are precisely the kinds of norms that Jesus challenged, again and again, as he walked his way into discovering where God is at work. He just "had to go through," not *around* the place that wasn't supposed to be on the map. Why Jesus *had* to go through isn't made clear at the outset, but the story that ensues opens up new possibilities for the surprising geography of grace. Who knew that this shamed, outcast Samaritan woman would in fact become a key person in the salvation and redemption of an entire Samaritan community, paving the way for cultural others to encounter the living God?

What's striking about this passage is the way in which Jesus goes right to the heart of the matter, while still recognizing the cultural tension that defined their social worlds. Jesus does not pretend to be colorblind when the Samaritan woman initially objects to their interaction; rather, he names their differences and yet engages on a deeper level. Jesus acknowledges their historic conflict and also reframes the whole story by pointing to the new work the Spirit is doing as God draws all people to himself.

Jesus could have easily said, "I don't see you as a Samaritan woman; you are simply an individual person, and I treat all people equally." A surface-level reading may even point to such thinking. But what if just the opposite is true? What if it is *because* she is a Samaritan woman that Jesus chose to meet her in her own neighborhood and demonstrate the expanding geography of God's plan to reconcile all people to one another? Jesus *had* to go through Samaria because that's where the path of discipleship leads: right into the places where historic, systemic racial conflicts have led to division and strife.

This kind of geographic transgression—this habitual crossing of color, class, and gender lines—is what continually characterizes Jesus' faithful ministry of inviting his followers to consider a new kind of belonging and a new kind of community that would embody this unusual belonging in the world. If we are going to work against "racial faith," or at least seek to follow Jesus more closely into the Samarias of our own cities and neighborhoods, then we will have to practice a Christian discipleship that is more attentive to the places and patterns of exclusion that divide our communities.

Jesus *had* to go through Samaria because that's where the path of discipleship leads: right into the places where historic, systemic racial conflicts have led to division and strife.

This task will not be easy. When the disciples—who had briefly run off to get groceries while Jesus was chatting it up with the Samaritan woman—returned to the scene, they were quite confused on a number of levels. Perhaps not knowing what else to do, they offered Jesus a bite to eat, but Jesus brushed them off for a teachable moment: "'My food,' said Jesus, 'is to do the will of him who sent me and to finish his work. Don't you have a saying, "It's still four months until harvest"? I tell you, open your eyes and look at the fields! They are ripe for harvest'" (Jn 4:34-35).

I wonder whether we, like the disciples, often find ourselves confused, hesitant, or disoriented when it comes to the strange places where God is working. Not knowing how to feel about the radical belonging Jesus practices, maybe we similarly look down at our food and wait in awkward silence. I believe Jesus is calling his church again, just as he did with the disciples that day in

Samaria, to open our eyes and look. The fields around us have been blighted by racial conflict and cultural tensions, but they are ripe for reaping the fruit of reconciliation. By the Spirit, Jesus is continuing to move into our Samarias. I hope we will respond to Jesus' invitation to follow.

- 3 -

From the Garden to the City

I've never been very good at gardening, and truth be told, I think I lack the patience and discipline that people need to cultivate a garden fruitfully. But in my limited gardening experience, it seems like an equally important ingredient for good gardening is the *desire* to really get in the dirt, till the soil with love, and care for a garden with an appreciation for the everyday miracles that occur when a plant grows, thrives, and bears fruit. The significance of this love for the dirt never really occurred to me until I noticed my son's affection for mud. He seems to be in his natural environment whenever there is a chance to dig, touch, feel, and *experience* soil, sand, water, and the many little creatures that make their home in the dirt. To me, prior to witnessing Jonas's fascination with the bits of earth he could grasp in his hands, the dirt was just dirt. But I've begun to think that perhaps a part of what I'm seeing in his love for the dirt is actually a deeper appreciation for creation—an understanding of the inherent goodness of the earth that God so lovingly forms, tends, and declares as "*very* good" (Gen 1:31). Could it be that the ground beneath our feet is more than just ordinary dirt?

The Physical Is Spiritual

Growing up in evangelicalism and being the faithful churchgoing, Sunday school–attending, youth group–leading kid that I was, I distinctly remember an overarching emphasis on the goodness of focusing on "eternal" things—particularly the bliss of heaven and the importance of ushering people into the "spiritual" realm. After all, so the thinking went, the earth and all of its worldly stuff was only temporary, and the *real* point of it all was the afterlife. If everything in this life is eventually passing away into an inevitable oblivion, then isn't it absolutely crucial to get people onto the life raft of salvation before this ship sinks into the abyss?

In no way am I trying to belittle that perspective from my upbringing, and I still appreciate the urgency and seriousness of recognizing that there's much more to this life than what we can see and experience in the here and now. However, as I've come to understand the importance of theology and geography, I also see the danger in an *over*emphasis on eternal or spiritual realities to the exclusion of the here and now. As Johnny Cash sang, it's possible to become "so heavenly minded you're no earthly good."[1] In the ancient world, a version of this thinking was called *Gnosticism*, and one basic tenet of its beliefs was that truly good and spiritual things were of another divine realm. Conversely, the physical, material world was an inherently flawed and broken place.

One result of this dualistic worldview was a kind of dichotomized spirituality, a perspective that sharply divided the spiritual from the physical. Though this is slightly oversimplified, the idea was that good, spiritual people should focus on the transcendent nature of immaterial things as opposed to the "fleshly" pursuits of the material world. While early Christianity wrestled with the pervasive dualism of a Hellenistic world, a kind of modern dualism persists in Christian faith and practice today.

Whether it's the escapist notions of the rapture or the contemporary critiques of environmental advocacy, many Christians remain relatively committed to the old idea that we needn't pay too much attention to this world—that the dirt is, well, just dirt. But the "spiritual stuff"—whatever that really means—is where it's really at.

This line of thinking results in two particular casualties of interrelated realities that we've been discussing from the beginning: the necessity of our bodies, and the significance of place. First, when we succumb to an overemphasis on spiritual things that reflexively deemphasizes physical things, then the first question we have to wrestle with is about our bodies. What in the world are our bodies for? Are they merely flesh suits holding our true spiritual selves until the afterlife? One of the earliest heresies about Jesus was that he was not *actually* human, but rather in some kind of human disguise, a sort of phony flesh suit that contained the pure spiritual essence of God underneath. This view, which came to be called *Docetism*, was eventually condemned by the early church councils that affirmed Jesus' true and fully embodied humanity somehow intertwined with his fully divine nature.

Though this essential Christian doctrine was settled long ago, many of us still seem to believe in a docetic Jesus, a God who wears his humanity very lightly and isn't *really* human like we are. One only needs to view the dozens of stilted, wooden characterizations of Jesus in film to see how we imagine Jesus walking, talking, and even at times dying with such calm and dignified manners. This fictional Jesus is so spiritual that he seems able to transcend his own body! Similarly, we at times imagine our own spiritual selves being separate from our physical bodies. Like the soul that floats out of its body in the emergency-room drama at the point of death, we think our spiritual nature is divided from our physical nature, and the cost is a theological devaluation of our bodies. A body becomes just some kind of fleshly thing, with the real treasure inside being our true essence, floating up to a disembodied heaven.

But this disembodied Christianity not only costs us our humanity in terms of our bodies; it also robs us of understanding how connected we are to the land, the earth, and the places that actually make us fully human. When our spiritual categories exclude or deemphasize the physical world and the goodness of our embodied lives, we neglect the holistic nature of what it means to be Christian *in* and *for* the world, and the tension of being *spiritual* people *with* physical bodies, not in spite of them. In short, it is only when we embrace the truly spiritual nature of our physical lives that we can integrate and make sense of our bodies inhabiting the places we live, work, play, and worship. We cannot understand the Christian story without its inherently material context, and to affirm anything less than the spiritual goodness of the physical world is to depart from the very heart of Christian reconciliation that must take our gardens and cities into account as we practice life together.

It is only when we embrace the truly spiritual nature of our physical lives that we can integrate and make sense of our bodies inhabiting the places we live, work, play, and worship.

For too long, too many Christians have seen geography as neutral, as if the places and environments that make us human are incidental to our spiritual responsibilities. We imagine we've just randomly landed somewhere, as if no one had any agency in shaping where we find ourselves. But what if the physical geography of our lives is inherently spiritual, and places are the vital context of discipleship? We need to recognize that places are never theologically neutral, and try as we may to spiritualize our lives apart from geography, we cannot separate what God has inherently joined together.

Theology of Geography

One of my favorite stories from Bob Lupton, who has written extensively on Christian Community Development for decades, is one in which he describes hearing a sermon about place. "Bloom where you are planted" was the repeated refrain, a reminder for Christians to be salt and light wherever they find themselves. Though he had heard the idea many times before, something bothered him this time.

> There was an assumption being made that God, fate, heredity, or something other than personal choice had placed us where we were living. Glancing around the congregation, I began to wonder by what coincidence most of my successful friends owned homes where they did. . . . Was it God who had decided that physicians and bankers should be planted among the wealthy? . . . I had a sinking feeling that where we were living had been determined by a long series of intentional, personal choices that were primarily influenced by our earning power.[2]

Lupton goes on to address a significant question that had been overlooked: Why are you planted where you are? In his critique of Christian neutrality in terms of location, Lupton suggests that many of us have bypassed an important process of self-reflection when it comes to geography. Namely, when it comes to locating our lives—residentially, vocationally, and socially—most of us have simply assumed that the natural course of things leads us to where we belong. But the reality is that particular priorities and choices are actually at work in this process. Specifically, convenience, comfort, and upward mobility are some of the primary drivers in that natural trajectory. It shouldn't surprise us that the undercurrent of those values is so powerful that we can be pulled along without even realizing that we've actually *chosen* to go along for the ride.

Going with the flow doesn't seem to be a choice if there's no obvious alternative to floating downstream in the channels of ethnic and socioeconomic homogeneity that so often characterize our lives together. So, like Lupton, I am concerned that our Christianity has long ago floated away from the idea that there's even a viable alternative to following the popular currents of urban geography such as white flight, suburban sprawl, and gentrification, each of which involve waves of people acting with socioeconomic self-interest. We've gone so far down the river, so to speak, that we can't even see how we got to where we are, and how far upstream the choices we made at each turn actually were. I suspect that for many of us, the geography of convenience and comfort has ruled our lives with countless little choices about commute times, amenities such as schools and shopping, and the intangible nuances of race and class consciousness that work powerfully below the surface of our everyday choices. Added together, the cumulative effect of those choices, combined with our civil religion of individual liberties, has made it seem like wherever we've located our lives is just the way things are, or maybe even the way things should be.

But what is the cost of this alleged neutrality when it comes to geography? Lupton insists that one of the most basic tasks of Christian discipleship, the call to love of neighbor, is obscured when we simply bloom where we are planted without asking why we're planted where we are. The flow of capital—both social and monetary—streams toward accumulation and security, not poverty and need. As we float downstream, slowly but surely, we become further and further removed from our neighbors so prioritized in God's kingdom—particularly the orphans, widows, and foreigners among us.[3] This is not to say that good neighbors aren't needed among the powerful and privileged; certainly wealth, poverty, and need are measured by more than our bank account balances. But to suggest that Christians don't have a particular calling—a special concern, if you will—for the materially poor and downtrodden would seem to neglect significant portions of the Law, the Prophets, and the Gospels.

The tension between blooming where we are—being faithful in our local communities, neighborhoods, and places of work—and asking how and why we came to choose to locate our lives in those places is not an either/or dichotomy that easily resolves. Because of the dynamic and multifaceted nature of how place works in our lives, it is a false choice to present the situation as one in which we must either uproot our lives to "follow Jesus into the ghetto" or simply stay where we are as allegedly apathetic, upwardly mobile consumer Christians. Reality, and geography for that matter, is much more complex than this binary mischaracterization. Although I certainly agree with the principles of Christian Community Development that emphasize the importance of location, specifically the intentional choice to locate or relocate our lives among the poor or underresourced, I want to be clear that this is not a simple, unilateral move that all Christians must embrace uncritically.

It is a false choice to present the situation as one in which we must either uproot our lives to "follow Jesus into the ghetto" or simply stay where we are as allegedly apathetic, upwardly mobile consumer Christians.

Much ink has been spilled over the past decade reminding people that an unreflective relocation to diverse, urban areas can result in many negative outcomes that evoke the painful legacy of imperialism. But this risk and complexity is not a justification for Christians to opt out of critical conversations about place and geography. For example, I am often asked by people who are considering a move whether it's ethically or theologically responsible to relocate to one place or another. My most common answer, unsatisfactory as it sounds, is that it depends. If we ask the question earnestly, then we have to be ready and willing to do some honest reflection about our motivations.

What's underneath our hopes and fears about a particular place? Perhaps for now it is sufficient to say that as we are being attentive to our current surroundings, the places that define our lives in this season, it is also essential to back up and look at the bigger picture in order to consider a few difficult questions.

First, how have I benefited from presuming that my choices about place are "normal"? In other words, what geographic choices have I made that may not be available to others in my community? This is a question about privilege. Many of us make assumptions about places—what they need, why they're good or bad—that are rooted in structures of race and class. What I see as a poor neighborhood may for others be a community with great pride in their history of resourcefulness.

Second, how should I understand the issues of injustice that shape the wider context of my city in terms of housing, education, and socioeconomic opportunity, and what role do I play in either contributing to those injustices or dismantling them? This is a tough one. Obviously, no one wants to think of themselves as contributing to systemic injustices, yet we must acknowledge how our geographic choices have real-life effects on the communities and opportunities of others. Wherever I root in a place, there are everyday ripple effects of time, money, and relationships that can move in the direction of justice and healing, or reinforce the status quo. When I choose to put my kids in a particular school, what is the net effect not only for their educational goals but also for the hopes and learning outcomes of their neighbors? If I really believe that equal access to quality education is a public good, then it serves both my own interests and those of the community to mobilize my resources, including my own children, in service to that good. To withhold my resources out of fear or selfishness only perpetuates patterns of inequity that drive the glaring achievement gaps in classrooms across the country.

Christian faithfulness to these geographic questions must move us beyond the illusion that we are passive, neutral consumers of place, helpless to change the systems of real estate and urban planning. In order to construct a faithful theology of place, retracing some geographic contours of the biblical narrative may bring some common threads of place into clearer view.

The Story of Israel

I suspect many of us have wondered about the lush paradise described in the early pages of the book of Genesis. What was the Garden of Eden like? How did Adam and Eve live there before it all fell apart? What strikes me about the creation narrative set in Eden is the very earthy, rooted, and intimate way that God interacts with this first place in the biblical story. At each creative turn, God's hands are in the muddy clay, lovingly forming every wild creature and bird in the sky from the dirt. Then, in a masterfully creative act, "the Lord God formed a man from the dust of the ground and breathed into his nostrils the breath of life" (Gen 2:7). Adam's body is in turn the creative material for Eve, and God's garden paradise seems complete.

Unfortunately, it doesn't take long for this first environment of nourishing rivers, fruit-bearing trees, and harmonious creatures to take a terrible turn. Because of human sin, the first family is banished from the place designed for flourishing, and their exile in the wilderness becomes a pattern of dislocation and readjustment that marks Israel's story again and again. No sooner had they put down roots than they were scattered abroad. Cain, who murders his brother Abel, is driven to wander eastward, and he becomes a city builder. But despite this persistent geographic migration, the presence of God's grace among God's people never departs.

In the midst of their brokenness and God's continued course corrections, the people of God somehow find their way, even as they find themselves rooting their communities in unusual places, from Babel to Canaan. Though it isn't obvious in each particular relocation, there is an overall trajectory to Israel's migration, and interestingly, it moves toward both the geographic and ethnic particularity of a tightly defined people in Jerusalem. As the story of Israel moves to Zion and eventually beyond, there is an arc to God's mission that is bound to the promises made to Abraham (Gen 12:3), that all peoples on the earth would be blessed *through* Israel.

As we noted in the first chapter, this chosenness of Israel, their *election* over against other peoples, is no small plot element in the larger story. How is God going to save the world? By calling, forming, and redeeming a particular people. But as the plot moves forward, we see a place and a people more and more narrowly defined in order to fulfill God's covenant with Abraham. It seems like a natural recipe for ethnocentrism and exclusion: God rescues a people, commands the people to be set apart (culturally and religiously), and then after they wander for some time, he instructs them to set up camp permanently in a Promised Land with a city on a hill. The place and the people are bound together for God's purposes: that "the peoples of the earth would flow to the holy city. . . . Jerusalem was to be 'the joy of the whole earth.'"[4]

Isaiah 2:2-3 describes Isaiah's vision of Zion, the mountain of the Lord:

In the last days
    the mountain of the LORD's temple will be established
        as the highest of the mountains;
    it will be exalted above the hills,
        and all nations will stream to it.

Many peoples will come and say,
    "Come, let us go up to the mountain of the LORD,
        to the temple of the God of Jacob.
    He will teach us his ways,
        so that we may walk in his paths."
    The law will go out from Zion,
        the word of the LORD from Jerusalem.

In this picture of God's rescue plan, it appears that Jerusalem, and its temple, where God's very presence dwells, is *the* place where God's particular people can find their salvation. All of Israel's story converges in the dirt of the temple mount, where God is drawing all people to holy ground. The location of the holy city is the centerpiece through which God's word radiates into the world. Or so it seems. Once again, as we noted in the first chapter, as Jesus eventually arrives on the scene, the whole story takes a dramatic and essential turn.

The Mission of God

Thankfully, Israel's story does not conclude at the geographic arrival of God's people in Jerusalem. The narrowly defined and ethnocentric election of Israel is not the end of God's mission to redeem the world. Rather, what comes to a head in the holy city is a great reversal of sorts—a point of convergence that actually serves as the beginning of a new and fulfilled story with a much wider cast of characters across varied places and geographies.

Although the earliest chapters of Isaiah point to a future convergence of the nations in Jerusalem, as the book unfolds we see Israel face the punishment and discipline of Yahweh for failing to be faithful because of both idolatry and injustice. Exile, just like banishment from Eden, is the result of a faithless Israel who cannot uphold their end of a loving covenant with God. But Yahweh is consistently gracious and compassionate, and by the time we get to the third major section of the book of Isaiah, a formerly exiled people are returning once again to Jerusalem, hoping once more to rebuild the city and honor God's promises to bless the nations.

Isaiah 56, a significant chapter in this turn of events, marks the beginning of this dramatic turning point in the mission of God. With an emphasis on salvation for "others," Isaiah chooses two interesting subsets of people whose faithfulness becomes the subject of God's blessing and saving work: foreigners and eunuchs. These outsiders were habitually excluded for any number of reasons—ethnic discrimination, physical blemishes, and other kinds of cultural marginalization. Yet here they are bound to Yahweh in love and specifically highlighted as chosen, for "these I will bring to my holy mountain and give them joy in my house of prayer" (Is 56:7). Instead of Jerusalem being a central place for exclusivity and ethnic particularity, the holiest of places in Israel seems to be turning toward the nations with a new sense of openness for the shifting cultural geography of God's people.

It is no accident that in each of the prophetic temple-cleansing scenes of the Synoptic Gospels, Jesus invokes the authority of this exact passage in Isaiah 56:7, "For my house will be called a house of prayer for all nations." As Jesus symbolically condemns the temple system and its abuses of exclusion, he also lays the foundation for a new way of understanding God's people and their relationship to place. Jesus' confrontation of the religious establishment in Jerusalem eventually leads to his death, but one of the most significant events in the wake of the crucifixion is when the temple curtain is torn in two. No longer is the holiest of places an exclusive space for the priestly elite or only those with the appropriate requirements of lineage and authority.

Quite to the contrary, the location of God's Spirit is loosed in the most surprising way: to now make God's home in the hearts and gathered community of God's reconstituted people. The apostle Paul's repeated exhortations that the Spirit now dwells in a new temple—in the lives of individual believers and in the collective body of believers—is a revelation of momentous proportions that remarkably shifts the geography of what becomes early Christianity. But what then are we to make of Jerusalem, the city of God? Once Jesus is resurrected and the Spirit is on the move, does that particular place no longer hold any significance in God's story?

The essential challenge is to see the work of Jesus as the *fulfillment* of Israel's story, not a point of divergence in which God's people depart from their earlier history.

The temptation of a false dichotomy regarding place is to separate the story into two chapters. The first chapter is the journey toward physical Jerusalem and ethnic exclusion, a land of promise but only for the few especially qualified. The second chapter is then the postresurrection story, in which place no longer matters because the temple curtain has been torn, freeing the Spirit to work in any and every place. Rather than dwelling on either of these limited options, the essential challenge of holding these chapters together is to see the work of Jesus as the *fulfillment* of Israel's story, not a point of divergence in which

God's people depart from their earlier history. Jesus is the bridge between the particularity of Jerusalem and the universality of God's presence in all the places where God's people dwell.

God's mission plays out in both chapters, and the more we work to hold them together, the more we see the connections between God's calling of a people *to* a place (gathering) and the dispersion of those people *from* that place into the world (scattering). Not coincidentally, gathering and scattering are two modes of the church's engagement with place in the world today: being called together, and then dispersed abroad. The beauty of the coherence of God's story is the way the Jerusalem metaphor develops as Isaiah moves toward the conclusion of God's justice and salvation in the world. In Isaiah 65, the prophet sees "new heavens and a new earth," a restored Jerusalem where God's people dwell in peace, wholeness, and joy. The character of this flourishing place is of course the exact language picked up in the book of Revelation at the very end of the biblical narrative.

Calling Urban Gardeners

In Revelation 21, the author sees "the Holy City, the new Jerusalem, coming down out of heaven from God. . . . And I heard a loud voice from the throne saying, 'Look! God's dwelling place is now among the people, and he will dwell with them'" (Rev 21:2-3). Just as God made a home for his people in Eden, God's eschatological city resembles the garden's beauty and restores its original purposes. In the center of the new Jerusalem is "the river of the water of life, as clear as crystal, flowing from the throne of God and of the Lamb down the middle of the great street of the city. On each side of the river stood the tree of life, bearing twelve crops of fruit, yielding its fruit every month. And the leaves of the tree are for the healing of the nations" (Rev

22:1-2). This restored Eden nourishes and heals *all* the people who dwell there, and the whole story has come full circle.

At the very center of the story, just like the river of life that heals the nations, is the living water of Jesus Christ, the enthroned Lamb of God, who "became flesh and made his dwelling among us" (Jn 1:14). Though God had taken up residence in Israel through the tabernacle, and later the temple in Jerusalem, it is the incarnate Jesus, who made his dwelling among us, that makes God's final dwelling place in the new Jerusalem possible. As we survey the larger story from the muddy and intimate creation in Eden to the episodes of exile that scatter God's people to and from Jerusalem, we can see the complexity of God's call to dwell in a place.

Today, the church faces a uniquely integrative task of cultivation and place making in the "new Jerusalems" we long to see in our cities and neighborhoods. After all, the new heavens and new earth are not only "pie in the sky" platitudes we should reserve for the afterlife. What might it look like for the whole people of God to take place seriously in today's cities and in our own particular communities? Three simple metaphors in this call to urban gardening are to *root, go,* and *water.*

Root. To *root* is to intentionally dig down into the local soil. Putting down good roots is the key to health, growth, and stability. As the Eden narrative demonstrates, a place designed for relational flourishing requires some mud on our hands. I love the image of the Creator God rolling up his sleeves and getting into the dirt to animate the life that fills that garden. God's gift of life isn't given at a distance, or in a sterile laboratory environment. God's people are connected to the earth and designed to live in a delicate symbiosis with the creation that nourishes them. Even though life in the garden is short-lived, we see the rootedness of God's people all throughout the larger biblical story.

Israel is constantly blooming where they are planted—making the best of their varied cultural geography, whether by growing in number under oppressive Egyptian rule or marrying and settling down in exile in Babylon. If you consider the long and arduous journey of God's people, it is full of detours, missteps, and the hardship of rocky terrain. Yet their resilience is remarkable and compelling, and we wonder what kept them moving, hoping, rooting, and then starting over again.

The challenge of course is that roots don't grow overnight, and they often hit difficult soil and face a lack of water or other essential nutrients. Churches and Christian communities that are seeking to root in a neighborhood must do much more than host an event for the community or research some demographic trends of their neighbors. Shallow roots disconnected from other root systems often shrivel and cannot sustain the long-term growth needed to bear real fruit. Too often, I've seen well-intentioned people show up in my neighborhood, drawn to its diverse and vibrant multiculturalism, saying all the right things about how much place matters to God and God's mission. Yet when the fruit doesn't show up on schedule, or when the expected crop of apples yields oranges, the garden is abandoned or neglected for so-called greener pastures.

Roots take time to grow; the best gardens are nurtured over many seasons, some with a fruitful harvest, and some with a less desirable crop. In my own successes and failures at putting down good, healthy roots in a particular place, I've learned that gardening is a group activity and not the work of a talented or charismatic individual with a green thumb. A few years ago, I visited the Muir Woods National Monument, an amazing forest full of soaring, majestic, old-growth redwoods. While there, I was surprised to learn that the root systems of many of these tall redwoods are actually quite shallow, going down only a few feet into the ground. What gives the trees their remarkable strength to survive winds, storms, and landslides is the breadth and interconnectedness of their roots, which branch out at a distance that far exceeds the size of their canopy and intertwine with the neighboring trees' roots. Together, they form an interdependent network whose collective strength as a root system far exceeds the capacity of any one particular tree to go down deep on its own. Groves of trees are, in the words of my friends at the Parish Collective, "rooted and linked," whereas individual trees, no matter their impressive appearance, are inherently exposed and at risk.

In my neighborhood, there's a fantastic summer leadership program called Urban Roots, which trains and develops emerging leaders to serve their particular communities while they explore issues of identity and purpose in the context of the broader city. In collaboration with several community development organizations and local ministries, young people are empowered to reach out to one another as they put down roots in the city. As they are mentored over time, they grow into servant-leaders who connect across cultural and generational boundaries for the good of their communities. Many Urban Roots alumni have invested deeply in places where I now have the privilege of reaping the fruit of their labor.

Successfully rooting in a place requires real friendship and partnership, and healthy community gardens bear the best fruit when linked neighbors depend on one another for the flourishing and common good we all desire. What's interesting about Israel's story is the way their attentiveness to the places and peoples they encountered linked them to others who were unfamiliar, or cultural others. We consistently see a unique role given to outsiders such as Hagar, Tamar, Rahab, and Ruth—all unlikely characters in God's story because of their social, economic, or cultural status. But their vital inclusion in salvation history reflects the surprising genealogy and character of God's people when they root and join their neighbors wherever they are planted.

Go. At first, to go may seem at odds with the call to root. How can one put down roots while on the move? This is the exact tension we see in the journey from the garden to the city. But as we look at Israel's story of gathering and scattering, the nomadic nature of God's people is not an endless, aimless wandering. Rather, there is a slow but steady biblical progression from the lush paradise of Eden to the city of Jerusalem. In order to be faithful to the mission of God while on the journey, Israel has to be willing to uproot and go whenever God's purposes are on the move.

From Abraham onward, there's a pilgrim or sojourner identity that marks God's people and God's story. Even as they commit to blooming in some hard places, they also commit to following Yahweh into the unknown promises of a land and a place that seems distant and farfetched. Whether tackling the risks of intimidating neighbors or the seeming uncertainties of God's material provision, the people of God keep moving and pressing into the places on the horizon God has for them.

This movement culminates in the settling, construction, and establishment of Jerusalem and the temple that marks God's territory and serves as a symbol of where Yahweh resides on the earth. And even though the Jerusalem-centric vision of God's mission does not play out in the way many expect it to, it is the urban vision of the *new* Jerusalem—a place where the garden and city converge—that carries the mission of God abroad into every corner of the known world of that time.

How should we understand the significance of the new Jerusalem for our own sense of place in the mission of God today? *Going* is not about traveling to the places that pique our curiosity or seem like a fun adventure; nor is it about exploring unknown geographies for the purpose of self-enrichment. In a Christian theology of place, going is in essence a response to being *sent.* When God asked Isaiah, "Whom shall I send? And who will go for us?" Isaiah simply replied, "Here am I. Send me!" (Is 6:8). This is a response of missional faithfulness. Ultimately, to go is an act of obedience to the *missio Dei*, the "sending-ness" of the triune God, who commissions the church into the world. Jesus put it most succinctly when he told his disciples, "'Peace be with you! As the Father has sent me, I am sending you.' And with that he breathed on them and said, 'Receive the Holy Spirit'" (Jn 20:21-22).

It's important to remember that going could consist of being sent near or far. In 1853 Hudson Taylor, a pioneering missionary to China, sailed for six months from Liverpool to Shanghai, where he traveled inland and committed to a life of ministry among the poor. In contrast, a generation prior Robert Raikes went just down the street to the jails and urban slums of Gloucester to teach illiterate children how to read in "Sunday schools" that would become a precursor to public education throughout England. Both were answering the call of the Spirit to go.

As the people of God respond in faithfulness to the sending of God, we are agents and instruments of God's peace and justice through the power of the Holy Spirit. Going to the new Jerusalem is not only an eschatological metaphor for the age to come, but it is a vision of God dwelling among all people in wholeness and goodness that mirrors both the beauty of the garden and the significance of the city. In this sense, the new Jerusalem is not only a destination; it is a place we pursue and cultivate in the here and now, as a sign of God's kingdom breaking into the present moment and our immediate geography.

And yet, even as we affirm the importance of God's reign independent of specific destinations, we must also be willing to journey toward the particular places right in front of us that are most in need of the healing God's presence brings. Why is the desire to go to Africa so much more common than discerning a call to African American communities in places like St. Louis? It would seem that few Christians feel called to a place like Ferguson, Missouri. Too many of our local communities and neighborhoods are broken and scarred by injustice, oppression, and violence. Tensions of race and class erupt in disturbing events that reveal deep pain and loss just below the surface. Festering wounds have gone unattended, and at times the generational cycles of poverty and marginalization feel too overwhelming to overcome.

We must be willing to journey toward the particular places right in front of us that are most in need of the healing God's presence brings.

I believe Yahweh continues to ask, "Whom shall I send? And who will go for us?" This is an invitation to follow the Spirit into the dark and difficult places of pain where injustice has bred bitterness, hopelessness, and self-destruction. Once again I'm reminded of God's people who did not shy away from the cold realities and harsh social divisions of the first-century world. The missionary movement that swept through the early church followed the Spirit into some low places and found deep wells of God's grace among the poor and excluded. Communities composed of oppressed slaves, marginalized foreigners, uneducated women, and all manner of improper and unacceptable people found a place of hospitality around the table set by the early followers of the Way.

Water. Finally, to *water* is the active nourishing of places in the midst of going and rooting. Christians must tap into the living water of the divine river that flows from God's throne through the heart of the new Jerusalem. That water is a current of refreshing sustenance for the heavenly city and all the nations that dwell there. As living water nourishes the tree of life, it bears healing fruit for all people. If your neighborhood were an urban garden, how would you characterize the fruit being born there? As you water your neighborhood, is it nurturing the local soil as it should?

Many insist that there is no clearer imperative in the Gospels than to "love the Lord your God" and "love your neighbor as yourself" (Mk 12:30-31). I don't think it's too presumptuous, then, to expect faithful Christians to be particularly good neighbors. Every once in a while, when my immediate neighbor is out of town, she asks us to water her garden while she's gone. It's hardly an inconvenience to make sure her plants and flowers are taken care of in her absence, but I wonder whether that's usually the extent of our neighborly courtesy when it comes to watering.

Many of the places we inhabit, and especially the urban places that shape our lives, are in need of the basic care and investment that keeps them hospitable environments for cultivation. Before they're even ready for a good watering, they could use some debris clearing, weeding, and even environmental restoration from dumping, pollution, and neglect. Too many of us, shaped by biases of individualism, see places as either public or private, and we presume that public places are maintained by institutions, and private places are cared for by responsible individuals. If a place is in disrepair or suffering from neglect, then we either alert the appropriate organization or chastise an individual as irresponsible. A "bad" place, therefore—whatever the problem may be—isn't my problem. It's someone *else*'s problem—someone who needs to take responsibility.

Christians must think differently about the demands of their heavenly citizenship. In the first few chapters of the book of Philippians, Paul uses this language to tease out the dual-natured ethics of early Christians in the Roman world. Though they had earthly obligations as citizens of the empire, their habitation in God's kingdom in the present also called them higher and further. As dual citizens of the worldly and heavenly city, Christians don't live compartmentalized, split-personality lives. Rather, they must live into the fullness of God's story, where the shalom of the new Jerusalem, a wholeness rooted in mutual flourishing, moves God's people to be good neighbors on a deeper level with a public and communal conscience.

In the early 2000s, when Grandview Calvary Baptist Church in Vancouver, British Columbia, began to renovate local housing that had fallen into disrepair, they faced many challenges of cyclical poverty and addiction in their underresourced urban neighborhood. But thanks to their faithful persistence and a commitment to genuine hospitality, they created spaces for flourishing that eventually caught the attention of the city of Vancouver. City leaders, long confounded by the challenges of the community, came to the leadership of Grandview and essentially said, "We don't know how you're doing it, but we can see the public good you are creating. Can you help us to understand how you're restoring the neighborhood?"

Neighborly watering of peace and justice is the natural outcome of Christians who understand that the places we inhabit are not simply public or private. Because we are bound to one another in a delicate and "inescapable network of mutuality," all places are inherently communal.[5] Cities especially highlight this fact, though we are often reluctant and shortsighted enough to avoid what's best for our neighbors as a whole. As we consider the complex work of urban gardening, and the rooting, going, and watering therein, I pray we will take more of Bob Lupton's words to heart:

> I have become persuaded that location, location, and location are indeed the critical selection criteria for those who desire to bloom where God has planted them. And the underlying values of those who perceive the Kingdom will be disclosed in the kind of questions they ask. What community lacks the talents and treasures that have been entrusted to us? What neighborhood will the unique leaven of our lives cause to rise? What school is most in need of the educational and moral values that our families bring? Location, perhaps more than any other decision, disturbs the delicate balance we have tried to achieve between mammon and spirit. In this issue, the American dream collides with the vision of God's Kingdom here on earth, exposing them to be as different from each other as darkness and light. Convenience, security, and status are confronted by self-sacrifice, downward mobility, and obedience.[6]

If God is indeed calling and forming a people, and these people are actively cultivating the fruit of the Spirit, where might God be planting them for the good of the city?

PART II

PATTERNS of EXCLUSION

Structures That Divide

- 4 -

Walls of Hostility

Once more Jesus put his hands on the man's eyes. Then his eyes were opened, his sight was restored, and he saw everything clearly.

MARK 8:25

Throughout high school, I worked in our family photo lab in Vancouver Mall, and on breaks I would walk around to see other store displays nearby. In the early to mid-'90s, there was a particular trend in a lot of the poster and gift shops, which would display large, patterned images with a "hidden 3D picture" out in front of the store. People walking by would stop and stare to try to find the hidden picture, some for just a few moments and others for much longer.

A fortunate few could see the three-dimensional image right away, and they would often smile or laugh when they discovered it. Others would become so frustrated because the only thing they could see was the flat, patterned background, totally unable to discern what was seemingly hidden right in front of their face. Some frustrated types even dismissed the illusion as a hoax, insisting that people were just imagining the hidden picture and playing along for social reasons. It was all quite fascinating to watch.

These computer-generated images are called *autostereograms* and use a visual illusion of depth perception to hide a three-dimensional image inside a two-dimensional pattern. Because of the ways our eyes are conditioned to look on the surface, at first most people just see the flat pattern and nothing more. One trick to seeing the hidden picture is to look *through* the pattern by shifting your point of focus behind the image, and then the 3D picture springs to life, often in a pleasantly surprising way. Once you've shifted your focus, the whole thing looks different: the pattern on the surface drops to the background, and the 3D image becomes the new subject and focal point.

When most of us look at cities—and their systems, structures, and patterns—I think there's something similar happening. Without the right perspective, the patterns look flat and rather meaningless. Sure, there's some vague familiarity with the general shape and layout of things (buildings, roads, people), but nothing really important or interesting stands out to us. Nothing grabs our attention, so we walk right on by, disregarding the pattern as insignificant.

"Patterns of exclusion"—structures that divide—can seem hidden at first. It may look like there's nothing there at all, but in fact there are outlines, contours, and images of something deeper going on. Housing, schools, transportation, social spaces, and more—together these patterns point to something more meaningful that may not leap off the page in an instant but can come into focus if we concentrate and know what we're looking for. These patterns are not only in the built environment, but they are also in our histories, social tendencies, hopes, and fears.

A Line in the Sand

Walls, fences, borders, and boundaries are all around us, and they generally serve a common set of purposes: to divide, define, and demarcate. Geographically, walls and boundaries can be very important for the design of the built environment or the standards of public safety. For example, I'm usually grateful for the fenced areas in parks where my young children play; they can run freely without the danger of cars, and their exploring can be contained lest they wander too far. But walls can also divide to the detriment of a place; borders can create tension over contested ground or exacerbate violence that builds on either side of a physical or metaphorical boundary.

While the ordinary walls among us mostly go unnoticed—a landscaped retaining wall or a friendly neighbor's fence—sadly, there is no shortage of the contested and divisive type of wall. For example, Donald Trump's well-publicized desire to build a huge wall along the Mexican-American border is only the latest proposal in a long history of wall building. These "walls of hostility," as the apostle Paul refers to the cultural divide between Jews and Gentiles, remain active and entrenched barriers in our world today. Some of them are more obviously constructed, such as the security wall around the Israeli West Bank (known as the "Apartheid Wall" by many Palestinians). But these days most of them are harder to see at first, especially when so many suggest these walls have all come down and are relics of an uglier history now past.

Many of the walls are both historic walls that have had lasting and unforeseen effects on their communities and invisible walls that have formed along racial and socioeconomic lines. Keep in mind that physical boundaries are not necessarily more imposing or damaging to the common good, though at first it may seem that way. In fact, many of the symbolic walls we face—cultural boundaries, color lines, class barriers—are actually

more dangerous to the flourishing of communities precisely because of their intangible characteristics. In a sense, it's their invisibility that protects and reinforces their power. When we fence a group in physically, the moral dilemma is clear. But when we create a boundary that's less apparent or obvious on the surface, its divisiveness may be contested.

Ultimately, as we identify and interpret these boundaries and the places they shape, I hope we bring the deeper meaning of these walls to bear on how the places we inhabit have in turn shaped us. If the church is ever going to summon the courage to transgress these walls of hostility, then we must understand the walls we're up against.

Road Tripping

When I was a kid, my family took a long, cross-country road trip from North Carolina to northern California. The adventure included stops at the eclectic Graceland in Memphis, Tennessee; the enormous Hoover Dam just outside Las Vegas, Nevada; and many places in between. From Elvis's vast television collection to the marvels of human engineering, there was lots of Americana to take in, but one of my most enduring memories is of the vast, expansive landscapes that we traversed by highway in our trusty Dodge Caravan. Crossing the country by car provides a lot of time to survey the varied geography that spans the great distance between two oceans.

If the church is ever going to summon the courage to transgress these walls of hostility, then we must understand the walls we're up against.

Not that long ago in the United States it was actually much more difficult to cross the country by car. Just a generation before, a long interstate road trip was a cultural novelty only made possible by one of the largest public works projects in US history: the Federal Aid Highway Act of 1956. This construction of a national interstate highway system literally paved the way for all sorts of new ways of exploring, inhabiting, and dividing the spaces and places where we live, work, and play.

The vast proliferation of highways not only made cars and the automotive industry a cultural and economic centerpiece of American society, but it also changed the scale of our daily lives. We could suddenly move faster, commute longer, and create new settlement spaces that were previously unimaginable, such as the suburban residential development or shopping mall. A prize of American ingenuity—going faster and farther, all the while fueling the engine of the economy—it's difficult to imagine anything could go wrong.

My Way or the Highway

While the benefits of highways in terms of transportation efficiency were significant—not least of which being national defense—many of the lasting effects of our highway systems were somewhat unanticipated. As is always the case with notable physical changes in the built environment, people tend to shape their lives around the geographic options made available to them, and this was certainly true for the tens of thousands of miles of highways that crisscrossed our states and cities like concrete and asphalt ribbons around the country.

While the process of building highways in and around cities was complex and multifaceted, these highways created new ways for cities to manage growth and development, especially in housing. Particularly in the population boom of the post–World War II era, the demand for more new housing was a pressing need for every city, and highways provided a natural course of development that would forever change the physical and cultural landscape of communities across the nation.

Prior to the existence of freeways, beltways, and expressways that made individual car transportation a way of life, housing in urban areas tended to cluster in higher-density neighborhoods. Space in cities was always at a premium, but with amenities like stores and jobs being centrally located, multifamily housing in tighter proximity made the most sense. Apartments, row homes, duplexes, and triplexes were intermingled with commercial or retail spaces, smaller single-family homes, and public spaces such as parks or community squares. This kind of geographic arrangement would later come to be known as a "traditional" neighborhood layout. Much of what was built in American cities in the first half of the twentieth century more or less resembled this kind of place in terms of the design of the built environment.

But highways, and their thousands of fast-moving, shiny automobiles, would eventually help to create a new, alternative kind of neighborhood that permanently redefined how Americans understood housing, space, and community: the suburbs. Suburbs were simply self-contained residential communities outside a more central urban area but connected to the city by highways. What began as the natural outcome of geographic and economic opportunity would deeply mark the urban landscape with the logic of race and place. It is probably safe to assume that suburban development did not set out to powerfully reshape societal notions of belonging, but as we examine how suburbs drastically restructured wealth and opportunity in the nation for generations to come, it is impossible to ignore the racially divisive results.

Suburban Bliss

Before I launch into a full critique of suburbia, it might be helpful to reiterate that I'm a product of suburban neighborhoods and the good schools and safe streets we commonly associate with the suburbs. Through much of my childhood, it was all I knew, and my experiences there fit with many of the stereotypical expectations of sheltered isolation. But suburban areas today are complex and fast changing, and it would be inaccurate and irresponsible to paint the suburbs with too broad a brush of privilege and homogeneity, especially given the fact that we've seen significant shifts in the demographics of many suburban areas over the past fifteen years or so, with notable increases in suburban diversity and poverty.

Yet at the same time, we must be honest about the very particular history of suburbia and the disturbing ways that suburbs created possibilities for many while explicitly excluding many others. Images and echoes of that exclusion are still prominent today for those with eyes to see and ears to hear. The burbs are not inherently evil, but the story of how they came to be is hardly an innocent tale. Quite tragically, the cultural and economic walls created by suburban growth and development are perhaps some of the most lasting and damaging barriers in our racially divided cities today.

Ignorance of this history may indeed be bliss because it bolsters the illusion we explored in chapter three, the fallacy that we are passive consumers of place, living above or apart from the land. But contrary to the notion that place is neutral and we all simply choose the kinds of places where we want to live, the development of suburbia is a clear example of how patterns of exclusion can create structural division. Geography has a long memory, and none of us got to where we are by random chance alone. As we look closer at the story of highways,

The cultural and economic walls created by suburban growth and development are perhaps some of the most lasting and damaging barriers in our racially divided cities today.

housing, and the walls created along the way, it will provide a clearer picture of the true cost of the suburban American dream and the challenges of Christian discipleship in the face of a racial faith.

8 Mile Road

In 2002, rising hip-hop star and talented rapper Eminem cemented his celebrity status with the film *8 Mile*, a huge box-office success that retold the story of Eminem's origins. Besides highlighting his humble beginnings as a poor white kid living on the wrong side of the tracks, the story put the hip-hop scene in Detroit on the map, with particular emphasis on 8 Mile Road, the historic dividing line between whites and blacks.

8 Mile Road, also known as M-102, is a Michigan highway that runs east-west along the northern border of the city of Detroit. Physically, it is simply one road in a system of many highways that run through the state. However, as we've explored from the beginning, the real meaning of a street sign like 8 Mile often transcends its physicality or material boundaries. But how exactly did 8 Mile Road achieve such cultural significance and notoriety? Unsurprisingly, it began with a wall.

Like a lot of other American cities, the population of Detroit grew significantly through the 1930s, and by 1940, new housing development had basically reached the northern edge of the city. Around the same time, the Federal Housing Administration (FHA), created by the US government in 1934, had begun to lay the foundation for homeownership as a central component of the national economy under Roosevelt's New Deal reforms. FHA-backed home loans essentially restructured and regulated the entire mortgage industry in order to make homeownership accessible and affordable for "all," especially for new home buyers in areas that would become suburbs.

As builders essentially ran out of space in Detroit, developers began to look more at the land outside the city, just north of 8 Mile Road. Mass-produced single-family homes were the newest (and most expensive) consumer item on the market, as the wave of the future toward prosperity and wealth had both government-backed financing and affordable, entry-level pricing with payment plans spaced over thirty years. It was an ingenious move on the part of the government to stimulate jobs, spending, and growth in the already prospering American economy. The land north of 8 Mile was ripe for development, and building new homes there would keep communities growing.

Redlining

But there was one big catch, and it was a significant one since it was determined by the color of your skin. Private developers needed FHA approval in order to finance their building projects, since it was FHA loans that would allow buyers to purchase their American dreams of white picket fences, cul-de-sacs, and suburban life. Without FHA financing, nothing built could be purchased, and so the FHA worked with the federally run Home Owners' Loan Corporation (HOLC) to establish a rating system for determining how and where housing loans should be prioritized. Explicit within this rating system was the racial makeup of the neighborhood, with subsequent consideration for where new homes could and should be built.

The underlying principle was quite simple: racially homogeneous *white* neighborhoods were stable and therefore good investments. Racially mixed neighborhoods were unstable and therefore a financial risk, depending on the particular ethnic ratios and the level of "black infiltration." Predominantly black or minority communities were deemed hazardous and therefore denied any potential investment. On HOLC maps, white neighborhoods were coded and outlined with the color green, the highest rating. Conversely, black and minority neighborhoods were outlined in red and given the lowest rating; they were "red-lined." Redlining was a common practice in FHA developments all across the country, and every city where people bought or built homes—from New York to Chicago to Los Angeles, and many places in between—was shaped by this blatantly racist policy. Following federal guidelines, the private banking industry also largely adopted the same methods of rating risk assessment.

Meanwhile, back in Detroit, when developers proposed some new construction on the north side of 8 Mile Road, and current residents also wanted new FHA mortgages, the racially coded rating system kicked in, and the maps showed that the proposed homes would be built too close to black communities on the south side of 8 Mile Road. Proximity to ethnic enclaves and racial diversity was too much of a financial risk, and applications for FHA loans would be denied. However, determined to build and profit, developers and residents had an idea: Why not build a wall to establish a clear boundary between the black families living on the south side of 8 Mile and the new, white communities being built nearby?

Accordingly, the 8 Mile Wall was built in 1940. About a half-mile long, six feet tall, and one foot thick, this concrete wall still stands today. On its completion, FHA-backed loans were approved on the other side of the wall, and new homes were built in suburban neighborhoods that quickly became exclusive white enclaves outside of the city. This pattern was not unique to Detroit, and all across the nation, suburban development took shape and amassed wealth on the essential foundation of racial exclusion. And as if the FHA's complicity in racist banking policy wasn't enough, private developers also played their part through a consistent use of racially restrictive housing covenants that explicitly excluded people of color from living in, renting, or purchasing homes in these new suburbs.

Legacy and Loss

Perhaps all this reads like a tragic but unsurprising history of pre–civil rights injustices related to housing and urban planning. Unfortunately, even though fair housing legislation passed in 1968, these discriminatory policies and divided communities are not a thing of the past.

First of all, the FHA's policies, in conjunction with private banks and developers, were allowed to operate legally with explicit racial exclusion for over three decades. That's a lot of time for people to buy homes and gain equity in an inherently imbalanced system. Imagine you were approved for a thirty-year mortgage in 1935. By 1965, your home loan would be paid off, and the house you purchased would most likely be your biggest financial asset or a resource to pass on to the next generation, or both. But what about the black families and other families of color who were denied access to both loans and homes? The math isn't complicated. Not only were families of color systematically excluded from the economic opportunity of homeownership, but their housing costs, typically in the form of rental payments, went directly to building the equity and wealth of white property owners.

Second, in 1968, when the Fair Housing Act passed outlawing housing discrimination based on race, color, or nationality, the available housing market was not transformed overnight. The damage had been done, and the shift of legal policy, while absolutely important, could not quickly undo more than three decades of racialized housing and the disproportionate accumulation of wealth. In fact, in nearly every city where racial diversity existed, state and local governments, supported by public opinion, resisted housing integration well into the 1970s, even though courts mandated fair housing again and again. It turns out that laws often change much more quickly than our personal prejudices and cultural biases.

So now that we're nearly fifty years past federal housing reforms, what progress have we made toward more equitable and integrated neighborhoods? Unfortunately, if we were to plot out the racial demographics of the nearly four million residents of metropolitan Detroit using data from both the 2010 Census and additional community surveys, we would see a haunting image of racial division. Today, the census tracts along the south side of 8 Mile Wall are more than 90 percent black, while many tracts on the north side of the wall are more than 80 percent white. Though the policies the wall once enforced have changed, the realities of racial division have endured. Detroit continues to face enormous challenges with concentrated, generational poverty, and gaping racial disparities in employment, education, and health care. Again, these figures are not from 1940, when the wall was built, or from 1970, right after fair-housing reforms. This is the most recent data available *today*.

How did this happen? What power did that little six-foot wall have to exert on millions of people more than seventy-five years later? The reality of course is that 8 Mile Wall in Detroit was and is much more than a concrete divider along the city's edge segregating black from white. Rather, the enduring legacy of the wall is a reflection of our collective fear of whomever we deem other and a physical manifestation of racial logic that questions whether or not we can live together. Christian belonging insists we can and should transgress the boundaries that divide us. But when we look at places like Detroit, and the mirror it holds to our racial fears, perhaps we have not fully taken into account how deeply the legacy of racism is embedded in our urban geography and by extension the very nature of our own consciousness.

Bringing It Home

Most of you do not live in Detroit, and it's likely you live in a place far less obviously segregated. But make no mistake: the absence of an 8 Mile Road in your own community certainly does not mean those walls of hostility don't exist. It's more likely that people share a unspoken agreement about the places where they do or do not belong. It's implicitly understood by people on both sides of the boundary, whether divided by race, class, or culture. These walls may be less visible and more permeable than concrete, but they are no less significant.

What's most interesting about urban segregation today is that by many measures, overall residential segregation by race in large metropolitan areas has decreased since the 1960s, aided in part by significant demographic shifts in the past fifty years. However, what is masked by the large scale of a metropolitan-level view is how *functionally separate* communities remain at the local level, whether block by block or neighborhood by neighborhood. It's in schools, churches, shopping malls, and "third places" (such as cafés, community centers, and parks) that our old racial prejudices steadily resurface. Much of the research that captures our everyday interactions, the composition of our social circles, and the places we frequent show that racial segregation is alive and well in nearly every city where we find different kinds of people allegedly living side-by-side. In fact, social statistician Nate Silver reminds us that our "most diverse cities are often the most segregated," as it's "all too common to live in a city with a wide variety of ethnic and racial groups—including Chicago, New York, and Baltimore—and yet remain isolated from those groups in a racially homogenous neighborhood."[1]

Some of this could naturally be explained by our social habits and patterns of comfort that always lean toward familiarity. Yet the degrees of inequality and segregation most cities face today by race and class are by all accounts severely contradictory to the desires for diversity and equality we all publicly profess. As a society, we seem to have decided long ago that the idea of "separate but equal" was a farce because of the inherent inequality of segregation. Yet when objections to integration of various forms continue to plague our schools, neighborhoods, and churches, politely updated versions of separate but equal are a common refrain. We insist that people prefer to self-segregate and rationalize that there's nothing wrong with preferring what's familiar.

As we look at the reality of segregation in our cities, how can we quantify the divisions between us? Let's consider just two measurements of racial segregation that can be tied back to the legacy of highways, suburbia, and segregated housing: housing wealth and school segregation. Each of these urban realities confronts us with an uncomfortable truth about how little has changed since the civil rights era.

Beginning with housing, it would be difficult to overstate the significance of the particular history of suburban economics. Because of FHA policies such as redlining and the geography of racial exclusion built into suburbia, during critical decades of growth in American wealth "most of the mortgages went to suburbanizing America, and [the FHA] suburbanized it racially. . . . Between 1934 and 1962, the federal government underwrote $120 billion in new housing. Less than 2% went to nonwhites."[2] Indeed, the suburban dream of owning a home was the cornerstone of upward mobility for an entire generation of Americans, but this dream was an exclusive one. For more than 98 percent of those who were given access to the dream and its rewards, a primary qualifier had nothing do with merit, work ethic, or ability. Rather, in this case, being born or labeled "white" was to inherit the privilege of access and the illusion of individually earned wealth.

According to the Pew Research Center, today the median household wealth of whites is thirteen to fifteen times higher than that of black households, and more than ten times higher than that of Hispanic households.[3] What accounts for this dramatic wealth disparity? To start, home equity and ownership is typically the largest financial asset in a household, but there is still a significant difference in white and black homeownership rates (73 percent vs. 45 percent).[4] So right out of the gate, the net worth of black households faces a notable disadvantage. Ultimately, the wealth gap widens along color lines largely because of *where* people live. In most cases, even when comparing white and black homeowners in the same city with the same education and income, a clear racial wealth disparity can most often be attributed to the contrasting values of their homes due to their different geographic locations. Sadly, the economics of place do not benefit all equally.

Today the median household wealth of whites is thirteen to fifteen times higher than that of black households, and more than ten times higher than that of Hispanic households.

Additionally, the stark residential segregation we see in most cities has another significant consequence: racial segregation in schools. In 2014, the Civil Rights Project at the University of California, Los Angeles, published a substantial report titled "Brown at 60," with a focus on the current state of public education in America six decades after the landmark ruling *Brown v. Board of Education* mandated racial desegregation in public schools. How much has actually changed since 1954? While the entirety of the research is complex, a few central ideas are clear. Although schools made notable progress toward racial integration in the initial decades after *Brown*, recent shifts have largely eliminated much or even all of that progress with only a few exceptions. Today, we must wrestle with why our nation has rejected the objectives of *Brown* and instead embraced the division, polarization, and inequities in our schools.[5]

In neighborhoods all across the nation, black children attend schools that are economically disadvantaged and racially homogeneous. More than 40 percent of black students attend a high-poverty school, which makes them six times more likely than white students to be in underresourced classrooms.[6] Additionally, nearly a third of black students are in high-poverty schools composed of 90 percent or more students of color. Research repeatedly emphasizes the fact that "poverty segregation in public schools tends to go hand-in-hand with racial segregation."[7] Tragically, the widespread reality of *separate and unequal* schools should not surprise us when we consider one of the primary funding sources of most public schools: residential property tax. With tax revenue based on separate and unequal home values, the disparate resources available to schools depend quite literally on their zip code. As we survey the landscape of our cities and suburbs, the historic and geographic pattern has come full circle.

First, political structures and banking practices were established to racialize housing and wealth. Next, segregated communities with disparate opportunities for socioeconomic mobility were created. Then, schools were built in those neighborhoods and were funded with tax revenues from the homes set up in the segregated system. So it should come as no surprise that from one generation to the next the inequities and divisions of race and class continue. Walls of hostility did not arbitrarily grow around individual prejudice or personal racism. Quite the contrary; these walls in our communities have been constructed, accepted, and even embraced throughout our society. And we have structured our very lives in the shape of the hostility resulting from the injustice of these walls. So what's a Christian to do in this walled and divided society?

Moving Toward Reconciliation

Up until now, I've mostly stayed away from more thoroughly unpacking the language of reconciliation, and that's been intentional. Though I am unquestionably committed to the theological premise that reconciliation—in all of its depth, complexity, and beauty—is at the center of the Christian story and the heart of the Christian life, I am also deeply concerned that we have at times moved too quickly toward the language and *idea* of reconciliation without truly wrestling with its meaning and consequences for our lives.

Sometimes when we are presented with a great injustice or a deep brokenness, like the kinds of division and segregation we've looked at in this chapter, we reflexively want to work on solutions right away. We often want to know how to fix the problem, implement the necessary change, and in so doing rid ourselves of the discomfort we feel at the ugly nature of injustice. We instinctively want the quick solution and the warm, fuzzy feelings that we associate with the ideas of forgiveness, reconciliation, and healing. But what if this shallow conception of reconciliation actually undermines the real work of reconciling by painting a false picture of the process?

Once again, Dr. Willie Jennings astutely offers an important caution in this regard: "Before we can interpret the depths of the divine action of reconciliation we must first articulate the profound deformities of Christian intimacy and identity in modernity.

. . . In truth, it is not at all clear that most Christians are ready to imagine reconciliation."[8] Though this is a hard truth to hear, I believe we must listen closely to Jennings's wise admonition. Before we move toward the mystery of God taking on flesh and the beauty of God joining creation in a radically self-giving act to restore the cosmos, we must pause and ponder the profound deformities of our failed attempts to live together as a body and a people. Too often, in spite of our many good intentions and claims of ignorance, we have passively and actively distorted belonging, abused our neighbors, and excluded the poor and vulnerable. In so doing, we have damaged not only those we are called to love but also ourselves in the process. We are not ready to imagine Christian belonging because we have not adequately plumbed the depths of exclusion, both in our own congregations and in the communities where we live.

So when we ask what we can do to become bridge builders and peacemakers in contexts of segregation, it is not so much a bad question as it is a premature one. Before we begin the fixing, perhaps it would be helpful to really consider the ugliness and brutality of the walls we've constructed and our own complicity in building and sustaining these walls. The realities of fear and hostility that fuel division also run through the middle of each of us and then get worked out in the places we cultivate and inhabit. We may not feel personally responsible for the walls of hostility around us, but we must recognize that many of us have benefited greatly from segregation at the cost of those who have been trampled underfoot.

We must recognize that many of us have benefited greatly from segregation at the cost of those who have been trampled underfoot.

We may want to debate how to best pick people up and dust them off, and this is an important piece of the conversation. But when the trampling happens again and again, year after year with devastating results, we may also want to ask: What in the world keeps crushing these people? And why has no one interrupted this repeated pattern of violence and injustice? If we are truly paying attention, then we must listen closely to the deep wounds of those whose dignity and personhood have been systematically dehumanized. A truly compassionate and unqualified recognition of the offense must precede any effort to simply fix a problem.

At the end of the day, reconciliation is always a slow and difficult-but-essential journey. Friend, colleague, and reconciliation guru Dr. Brenda Salter McNeil describes this journey as an "ongoing spiritual process . . . that restores broken relationships and systems."[9] Her circular roadmap metaphor is an important reminder that the *ongoing* nature of the journey to reconciliation is not a singular path with a terminal destination. Quite to the contrary, a commitment to this spiritual process is a long, transformative journey of "realization, identification, preparation, and activation."[10] Each phase moves us onward, but rarely with clear delineations. Pit stops and detours along the way are par for the course, and we should adjust our expectations accordingly.

When it comes to the walls we've built and the lives we've shaped around racial logic, we can't just knock them down by getting it done quickly or easily. Even as we've affirmed the remarkable ability of the Spirit-empowered church to cross boundaries and create belonging, we've also decried the church's cultural captivity, which cripples the gospel work of reconciliation. As we return to a picture of reconciliation in the early church described by the apostle Paul, I hope we'll hold in tension the genuine desire to move toward healing and belonging, and the real challenges of reimagining our lives together with God and one another.

Breaking It Down

Growing up, I used to get into a lot of petty fights and arguments with my younger sister. My specific memories of what exactly came between us so often have faded in adulthood, but I can recall a mediation technique my parents would often employ in an attempt to resolve our frequent sibling spats. "There's no one closer than siblings," they would say. "Brothers and sisters share a common bond that's very special." My dad would then explain how the children parents create have a shared lineage and therefore a shared identity. In a sense, this was a simple appeal to the nature of family: "You're siblings, so act like it!" But on a deeper level, this is also a kind of origins story that determines the shape and character of community and the necessity of recalling shared history in the midst of conflict.

In the second chapter of Ephesians, Paul addresses the church in Ephesus with a bold but pastoral concern about life together in God, which was increasingly tenuous as Jews and Gentiles were negotiating cultural conflict. He begins, as he often does, by reaffirming the salvation story, with Christ at the center. And even as he assures the church that "it is by grace you have been saved, through faith—and this is not from yourselves, it is the gift of God" (Eph 2:8), Paul then immediately reminds them: "For we are God's handiwork, created in Christ Jesus to do good works, which God prepared in advance for us to do" (Eph 2:10). This is all setup for the meat of the chapter, which lays out a challenge to the Gentile outsiders: "Therefore, remember that . . . you were separate from Christ, excluded from citizenship in Israel and foreigners to the covenants of the promise, without hope and without God in the world. But now in Christ Jesus you who once were far away have been brought near by the blood of Christ" (Eph 2:11-13).

Lest the church forget their former exclusion and what Christ has accomplished, Paul then cuts straight to the heart of the matter:

> For he himself is our peace, who has made the two groups one and has destroyed the barrier, the dividing wall of hostility, by setting aside in his flesh the law with its commands and regulations. His purpose was to create in himself one new humanity out of the two, thus making peace, and in one body to reconcile both of them to God through the cross, by which he put to death their hostility. (Eph 2:14-16)

In this vivid picture of peacemaking, Paul's incarnational language is striking: Christ, in the flesh, has *become our peace*, and in so doing he has destroyed the walls of division and hostility between the supposed insiders and outsiders, between the chosen ones and the unclean ones. In his very body, Jesus creates "in himself one new humanity out of the two, thus making peace" (Eph 2:15) and brings mutually excluded people together through the death of their own fear and hatred. It is the hostility of the cross that crucifies the hostility of human exclusion, and Jesus takes on the sin of segregation to re-create a new people.

Subsequently, by the work of the Spirit (Eph 2:18), we all

> are no longer foreigners and strangers, but fellow citizens with God's people and also members of his household, built on the foundation of the apostles and prophets, with Christ Jesus himself as the chief cornerstone. In him the whole building is joined together and rises to become a holy temple in the Lord. And in him you too are being built together to become a dwelling in which God lives by his Spirit. (Eph 2:19-22)

Thanks be to God! It is a remarkable depiction of God's creativity and compassion to imagine a divided people who are no longer estranged, a community where God is quite literally "forming a family out of strangers" and constructing a dwelling place for the Spirit.[11]

But before we call it a day by simply citing the authority of Scripture and moving forward, I think it is important to set this pastoral exhortation in context in order to sit with what it may really mean for us. Surely the rich metaphors of reconciliation in Christ's body and the destruction of walled hostility should prompt a collective "come to Jesus" moment. I believe we need those moments of truth and conviction over and over again in our journey of discipleship.

Yet even as Paul speaks in the present tense about what Christ has *already* accomplished in making peace in the place of hostility and belonging in place of exclusion, there was also a very real sense in which the social reality of the church had *not yet* lived into its calling to exemplify this new kind of reconciled family. Letter after letter of Paul's many epistles reveals that he knew all too well how the divisions of race, class, and gender permeated the cultural fabric of the early church. The real hostilities and hierarchies between groups were ongoing obstacles to the church's unity and public witness. Though Christ has indeed made one new humanity into a dwelling place for the Spirit, the details and practices of the process are easier said than done.

In my earlier example of arguing with my sister, it's not as if on hearing my parents' routine appeal to family we suddenly slapped our foreheads in a momentary lapse of memory. We hadn't simply forgotten our sibling connection and acted out of relational amnesia. Rather, we already knew the story but still struggled to realize its implications in the present, especially when tangible conflict would arise in the moment. Even after we were forced into an obligatory hug, the work of truly reconciling would take much more time and effort. And I'm happy to report that the childhood bickering between my sister and me is now a distant and humorous memory.

Christian reconciliation is a divine *and* human process, and the bricks that went into building the walls of hostility sometimes need to be carefully loosened and removed one by one. In God's economy, Christ has already done the work and destroyed the barrier, but our human participation in that work still requires patience and intentionality. As much as I want the beauty and immediacy of the incarnation to inspire our commitment to the ministry of reconciliation, I also want to have a deeper understanding of how massive and entrenched the walls of racial exclusion are in our midst. If we underestimate the wall, then we risk the danger of cheapening the work of reconciliation by glossing over the division. Instead of excavating the foundation to bring it down, we may simply chip a few pieces off the top, and this accomplishes very little.

> **Christ has already done the work and destroyed the barrier, but our human participation in that work still requires patience and intentionality.**

To really get at the root of the problem, we have to continue to dig a bit deeper.

- 5 -

Place, Parish, and Ghetto

My beloved city of Seattle was named after the indigenous leader Chief Sealth in 1853, whose Duwamish name, "Si'ahl," is an ironic and for many painful symbol of how this city was "settled" many years ago. The language of settlement subtly implies that the land was previously *un*settled, but as was the case throughout the Americas and especially in the westward expansion of the United States, the lands that would eventually become established territories were hardly uninhabited places. Tragically, the patterns of occupation, colonization, and displacement were repeatedly enabled by land grabs, violated treaties, and violence. There is no glossing over this ugly history as we consider how the places in our cities came to be.

Esteemed Nigerian novelist Chinua Achebe famously said that "until lions have their own historians, the history of the hunt will always glorify the hunter."[1] This variation on history being written by the victors is certainly true of Seattle. As white settlers "discovered" the rich natural resources and beautiful landscapes of the Puget Sound, wave after wave of opportunists and entrepreneurs arrived on the shores of Elliott Bay, the scenic waterfront area that today frames the skyline of downtown Seattle's bustling and fast-growing metropolis.

But the shores they landed on were already teeming with life and activity. By the early nineteenth century, more than a dozen indigenous communities of Native Americans made their homes in the land that would eventually become "Seattle." The Duwamish, Suquamish, Salish, and other tribes enjoyed the mild climate, proximity to lumber and fishing, and the various amenities that made their land such prime real estate. Chief Sealth, who advocated for peaceful relations with the whites, was a prominent leader among the Native communities who initially befriended some of the early settlers. But over time, slowly but surely, as a growing Seattle continued to attract more and more white settlers, Native communities lost their homelands and the places for community they had built there.

After the 1856 Battle of Seattle, a one-day skirmish between US Navy–backed settlers and Native American "aggressors," things took a turn for the worse. By the early 1860s, roughly half of the Native American population in the region had been either wiped out by smallpox or other related epidemics, or displaced to distant reservation lands. Duplicitous treaties made with the territorial governor were not honored, and whites encroached on prime real estate without consequence, all while continuing to restrict and regulate Native ways of life. In 1866, Chief Sealth, long relegated to a Suquamish reservation, died far outside the city that bore his name.

Seattle hip-hop duo Blue Scholars describes the irony this way:

This city was built on the backs of the brave
Who gave up their homes for a dollar a day
The same folks who rose up, demanded minimum wage
Unofficial slaves not given a page
A photograph or a paragraph written to claim them

Some got the nerve to say go back to where you came from
Same ones who stole the land from Chief Sealth
And then named the city after him
As if to say we honor you
Right after we conquered you and pillaged your home
Soil fertilized with indigenous bones.[2]

Today, as Seattle's beautiful landscapes and strong economy continue to make it one of the fastest-growing cities in the nation, the geography of Elliott Bay bears little resemblance to the clusters of Native fishing communities that once were. The streets of the downtown core are named after all the founding families of settlers—Denny, Yesler, and Maynard. But far below the towering skyscrapers that are now filled with new waves of opportunists and entrepreneurs—tech startups and cultural innovators—is a bloody history, obscured by the victors' symbolic triumphs of steel and glass. The soil is indeed "fertilized with indigenous bones," a faint reminder of the Darwinian nature of cities. Must only the strong survive?

Today, Chief Sealth's Duwamish peoples, who are now scattered throughout western Washington, are still struggling to negotiate with the descendants of the white settlers who came ashore so long ago. Despite ceding their vital Elliott Bay real estate to the territorial government in 1855, the now-infamous Treaty of Point Elliott curiously overlooked the Duwamish tribe and failed to secure any reservation lands for them. Ongoing requests and proposals for a Duwamish reservation in the subsequent years were continually blocked, declined, or denied.

Finally, after decades of legal battles and court appeals for federal recognition, in 2015 the US Department of the Interior issued a "final decision" in denying Duwamish tribe any federal recognition.[3] Of the many indignities the Duwamish have faced—including the Duwamish river corridor becoming one of the most industrially polluted waterways in the country—is a permanent exclusion from federal funding for land, housing, education, and health care. In exchange for his precious land and peaceful negotiation, Chief Sealth and the Duwamish were left with very little.

Place Matters

Hopefully by now we've established a few foundational ideas to build on: First, that place matters and is not a secondary consideration in the Christian life. Discipleship always gets worked out in our geography and must therefore take the physical contexts of streets and neighborhoods seriously. Second, we've looked at how race is a systemic reality all around us, a social construction woven into the places that shape our lives and our sense of belonging. Third, we've explored how patterns of history and walls of hostility have inscribed a kind of structural exclusion on the landscape of our cities.

Taking each of these ideas into account, it's essential to press further into some of the current issues that continue to illustrate how racial logic has been built into the urban environment. In doing so, the goal is not only to expose the patterns and connections that reinforce exclusion but also to reflect on the meaningful challenges that those in urban ministry face. The constructive work of equipping the church with tools and means to cultivate places of peace in the city first requires a deeper understanding of how divisive urban realities are not only problematic in places like Detroit, Ferguson, or Baltimore.

As we explored in the last chapter, the fears, tendencies, and policies that lead to segregation and hostility are universal to wherever people have to share space and find a way to live together. The details and settings may vary, but the outcomes are largely the same: left to our own devices, we congregate in pockets of homogeneity and seek the benefit of "our own." Then geography does the work of division that fragments and isolates communities.

So the challenge for the people of God remains: Will Christians follow these patterns of exclusion or disrupt them? Will churches reinforce segregation or work against it? I believe Christian communities, and especially those engaged in urban ministry, have a unique opportunity to practice and model meaningful, lasting reconciliation work. But the viability and effectiveness of this work will hinge on much more than idealism, analysis, and rhetoric. As we continue to examine barriers and color lines, I hope our willingness to listen, lament, and engage will also be bolstered by our resolve to act.

In that process, the interrelated themes of *place*, *parish*, and *ghetto* will present some challenges and opportunities for those who are seeking the peace and wholeness of the city. As usual, *place* forces us to dig into the history and geography of the land. How did these places come to be, and at what cost were they "developed"? *Parish* presents an ecclesial hermeneutic—a lens for the church—as a pastoral and incarnational presence in these places. *Ghettos* confront us with the persistent problem of isolation and exclusion that segregated places always face. Somewhere in between these challenges and opportunities is a called and sent people who must navigate this complex terrain with attentiveness and care.

Will Christians follow these patterns of exclusion or disrupt them? Will churches reinforce segregation or work against it?

As we've repeatedly seen in various places, land and geography are much more than dirt and space. In addition to framing how we understand where we're from and who we are, the places that provide vital contexts for our lives also carry significant capital—social, political, and economic. Land is a near-universal asset in this world, and private land ownership is an essential principle in capitalism. As such, the competition for land—and its subsequent division, development, and protection—fuels both conflict and economic growth on a massive scale.

So naturally, whenever we consider the aspects of place that shape our lives, we never do so in an ethical or theological vacuum. Land always tells a story of power and wealth, and whatever stories of community, belonging, or exclusion occur on that land are always layered over and interconnected with the politics and economics of the land. As we just explored in the case of the Duwamish, their displacement from the land was only the first step in the gradual erosion of their collective history and identity.

Taking the Best Meat

Some might suggest that at least many of the Duwamish escaped with their lives, which is more than you could say for many other Native American tribal communities, but the illegal occupation of Native lands and the resulting displacement of Native peoples was not without additional consequences. In reality, reservations—initially proposed as a way to preserve and protect Native ways of life from the outside world—turned out to be walls that kept settlers out and indigenous peoples in.

As photojournalist and Lakota activist Aaron Huey reminds us, the great tragedy of genocide occurs not only in the immediate brutality of violence but also in the painful aftermath of trauma and recovery.[4] The Pine Ridge Reservation in South Dakota is where the Lakota Sioux were mercilessly slaughtered in 1890 by US Calvary troops in the Wounded Knee Massacre. These soldiers were awarded at least twenty Congressional

Medals of Honor for the indiscriminate murder of children, women, and men at hands of the rapid-fire Hotchkiss gun. But as heinous and heartbreaking as this mass execution was and is, the real legacy of their deaths is the lasting dysfunction and societal brokenness that persists on the Pine Ridge Reservation today.

At Pine Ridge, as in many other reservations, the rates of abject poverty, unemployment, homelessness, preventable diseases, alcoholism, gang violence, family abuse, and other socioeconomic maladies are simply unthinkable. Many human development indicators such as infant mortality and life expectancy are comparable to war-torn Afghanistan, Somalia, and Iraq. What accounts for this ongoing echo of pain and loss that plagues so many Native communities right in our own backyards?

Wasichu is a Lakota word that means "non-Native" but can also be translated as "the one who takes the best meat." Huey offers this explanation:

> The last chapter in any successful genocide is the one in which the oppressor can remove their hands and say, "My God, what are these people doing to themselves? They're killing each other. They're killing themselves while we watch them die." This is how we came to own these United States. This is the legacy of manifest destiny. Prisoners are still born into prisoner-of-war camps long after the guards are gone. These are the bones left after the best meat has been taken. A long time ago, a series of events was set in motion by a people who look like me, by *wasichu*, eager to take the land and the water and the gold in the hills. Those events led to a domino effect that has yet to end.[5]

Painful as it may be to connect the dots, it should not surprise us that the patterns of exclusion and division that marginalized and isolated Native communities have resulted in such widespread catastrophe for Native peoples. And while we can certainly have a conversation about personal or individual agency, responsibility, and accountability, we can never separate such debates from their historic contexts of violence and the dysfunctions of dependency that grow out of systemic abuses of power.

The geographic and theological questions for those now occupying the land taken from indigenous peoples are complex. What could justice and reparation look like in places with a long history of violent confrontation and theft? How long and to what degree should our memory of past wrongs shape current policy? While we have models of Truth and Reconciliation Commissions in places such as South Africa, Canada, and Peru, the hope of recovering the idea and practices of a *parish* is that the church can play a role in restoring and remaking places of trauma into communities of peace.

A Chief Seattle Parish

In 1970 Father Raymond Talbott, a Jesuit missionary priest, noticed how many Native American people were living on the streets of Seattle and struggling to meet their basic needs. In cooperation with Native people in the community, he founded the Chief Seattle Club, whose mission is "to create a welcoming place of support, acceptance and ceremony for Seattle's native population."[6] With years of experience working among Native American tribes in the Pacific Northwest, Talbott understood the importance of creating "a safe and sacred place to rest, revive and nurture the spirit of urban Native peoples in need. We believe in the power of our ancestral ways, and preserving them means fostering a sense of community among those without one to call their own."[7]

Today the Chief Seattle Club, which remains a relatively small nonprofit organization, is located just a couple of blocks from the downtown Seattle waterfront on Elliott Bay, in the historic Pioneer Square neighborhood where a few small monuments pay tribute to early Seattle history. Interestingly, their exact location is right across the street from the Seattle Union Gospel Mission Men's Shelter, and just south of Yesler Way, which is essentially Seattle's version of an 8 Mile Road. The place where poor and homeless people from the Native community receive care is also the place where other frontline ministries of mercy have located themselves, right along the boundary line that divides the predominantly white and upwardly mobile north Seattle from the much more ethnically and socioeconomically diverse south Seattle.

What does it mean to be the church in a place like this, amid such tension, complexity, and contrasts? How can the people of God become more intentionally present to these urban challenges, both geographically and spiritually? Without reducing the solutions to three convenient bullet points, here are a few directions or trajectories the church can pursue to better listen, lament, and engage. Both the orientation and the destination are important in the overall process, but these suggestions are like *postures of place*: ways to position and locate ourselves in the shape of Christian faithfulness.

Listening Locally

Perhaps it is stating the obvious to suggest that listening is a critical practice in any form of Christian ministry, but unfortunately, when it comes to challenging contemporary issues, it often seems that analysis and argumentation precede any genuine desire to openly invite others—especially those at the center of the issue—to share their experiences and perspectives.

For example, in Seattle there is no shortage of opinions on homelessness, from the endless debates over policies and funding to the public wrangling over panhandling, tent cities, and potential best practices.

Yet the church is uniquely positioned to offer a different approach to the issues because its people-centric orientation is fundamentally human. Homelessness is about particular people created in the divine *imago Dei*, beloved with dignity, beauty, and agency. They are created with the gifts *and* imperfections of ethnicity, culture, language, personality, and personhood. And when the church is most faithfully the church, then the listening to one another that occurs in Christian community grows out of authentic relationships and belonging.

To borrow a concise definition from *The New Parish*, a *parish* is simply "all the relationships (including the land) where the local church lives out its faith together."[8] Identifying the land as essential to our relationality is actually an old strategy that recognizes how people can only listen to one another closely when they share the same geography. Community by proximity was not always novel; through much of human history it was necessity. *Listening locally*, then, is simply a return to that old but good practice of being an authentic neighbor, being present and attentive to those in our midst, especially those who—like orphans, widows, and foreigners—may need a good neighbor.

When the church is most faithfully the church, then the listening to one another that occurs in Christian community grows out of authentic relationships and belonging.

Father Talbott befriended and listened to the people in the Native community he met, and he responded to their felt needs—for sacred space, for the intimacy of speaking their mother tongue, and the basic affirmation and dignity that comes with food, shelter, and hygiene. The Chief Seattle Club became a place of belonging for Native people who had been cast off and chewed up by a society of settlers, and today it's an urban refuge for those whose personhood has been degraded by years of invisibility and abuse. Today their work of listening and neighboring continues faithfully, in the same way that listening to the community and responding to felt needs remain as foundational principles of Christian Community Development.[9]

As the church embraces its identity as a *placed* people, and not simply a building or a set of programs, listening locally becomes a fundamental practice of a parish whose posture is oriented toward the people in the neighborhood. Authentic listening requires honesty before God and one another, and intentionally prioritizes patience and personal connection over judgment, defensiveness, and "problem solving." The more local a parish becomes, the more listening becomes a natural byproduct of friendship and mutuality. Christians listen not for a particular result or outcome but because in being fully present to one another by the Spirit, we see each other in the image of community for which we were created.

Lament Compassionately

As we listen to one another, particularly in places of pain and division, we must also learn to move toward *compassionate lament* as a practice that lays the groundwork for solidarity, trust, and action. Simply put, "lament is the language of suffering."[10] The root meaning of compassion is to *suffer with* as an active participant, not to simply feel guilty as a passive observer. Sadly, many of us today face a kind of compassion fatigue as we are bombarded with local and global injustices that seem unending and intractable. In the face of such overwhelming needs, patterns of exclusion may feel like yet another injustice on the list—just one more issue to address in our broken world.

But once again, when the church adopts a parish-oriented posture toward the world, its immediate physical context provides some natural geographic guidance as the people of God discern their neighborly calling. Compassion for our neighbors grows not out of some forced, artificial sense of guilt or charity, but instead from the common experience of shared space, place, and life together. Drawing again on the basic affirmations of Christian Community Development, when the people of God locate their lives among hurting people there is no *them* when it comes to pain or injustice.[11] There is just *us* and our collective sense of shared tragedy or triumph.

Thus, compassion grows naturally out of loving our neighbors *as ourselves* instead of loving acquaintances just because Christians are supposed to. Genuine love of neighbor enables us to see people more fully and to understand their suffering beyond the well-intentioned but distant sympathy that plagues so much of our apathy and inaction. Only when we are truly present to our neighbors in a place, committed to authentic listening, and moving toward shared suffering can we enter into the seemingly strange and unfamiliar space of lament.

Lament as a deeply Christian practice is largely misunderstood in the Western and North American church, for various reasons that we'll explore more fully in part three of the book, but for now it is sufficient to say that we must grow more comfortable with the discomfort of voicing and embracing the visceral and unresolved nature of lament. In the Christian tradition, lament is both *cathartic* and *prophetic*, two essential realities we see proclaimed through the Psalms and Prophets in Scripture. To lament is to cry out to God and call attention to injustice and pain. And while its value cannot be measured or quantified like attendance numbers or program dollars, compassionate lament is an absolutely integral practice for parishes that choose to locate themselves in communities where structural exclusion has been woven into the landscape.

What, then, might lament look like for the landless in Seattle? For the Duwamish, perhaps it means we should continue to listen patiently to their decades of struggle and histories of injustice. We should not grow weary of "having this conversation again," but instead should ask ourselves more honestly, "Why do we continually avoid, minimize, and rationalize this history?" When asked to honor the sacred lands of Seattle, and the indigenous peoples who cultivated and protected the land for generations, we should reflect in sorrowful remorse instead of being dismissive of the exercise as a political charade. When presented with opportunities to right historical wrongs, we should enter with resolve into the sufferings of the past that remain in the present and offer empathic kindness, not shallow platitudes. Compassionate lament may not look like much on paper, but without its foundation, action remains disconnected from neighborly love.

Compassionate lament is an absolutely integral practice for parishes that choose to locate themselves in communities where structural exclusion has been woven into the landscape.

Engage Collaboratively

Collaboration may be another obvious or overused idea in community engagement, but its necessity is rooted in humility and partnership, not simply the marketing jargon of social change. Collaborative engagement is also an essential posture for those seeking to move from an attractional church (a building/program-centric congregation) to a parish approach. Too many churches and ministries leapfrog the practices of listening and lamenting in order to jump right into the missional stuff of community engagement, and the results can be disastrous.

Evangelical church-growth literature has been increasingly critical of attractional, megachurch approaches that adopt (either intentionally or inadvertently) a placeless or geographically neutral position about their location—and rightfully so. But an unintended consequence of many supposed missional communities (or whatever term people use to rebrand small groups), especially in urban neighborhoods where disparities of power and privilege are more pronounced, is the same dilemma and conflict that has perpetually discredited some missionary work: inadvertent ethnocentrism and cultural imperialism.

When churches move too quickly to adopt parish principles at the cost of long and patient listening and lament, their incarnational work, however well-intentioned, may be more messianic than they intend. Whether the issue du jour is homelessness, human trafficking, Native peoples on "the rez," or immigrants in the ghetto, I've witnessed firsthand the unintentional cultural imperialism that comes from the bad combination of eagerness and a lack of thoughtful preparation. When neighborhood outreach becomes the local equivalent of short-term mission trips to the so-called third world, the potential to actually hurt those we intend to help becomes more damaging than we realize. I sometimes call this *rescue without relationship*, an approach loaded with ethnocentrism and cultural superiority that can completely undermine the genuine desire and good intentions many Christians have to love their neighbors.

So what does genuinely collaborative community engagement that is rooted in humility and partnership actually look like for parish-minded Christians? There isn't a one-size-fits-all solution, but I continue to notice an entrepreneurial impulse that concerns me. Turning once again to my own neighborhood, in my roughly ten years of having coffee conversations with would-be church planters, community starters, and missional practitioners, I've had plenty of good discussions about diversity, place, and reconciliation. I'm grateful for many of the people who have come and gone, as well as those who remain in the community doing meaningful multicultural work.

Yet it's curious to me that I have never once, not in over a decade, heard an individual or group suggest that joining an existing ethnic church or predominantly immigrant congregation (or any church with a culturally dominant group different from their own) could be a powerful and transformative way to root in a place and practice the ministry of reconciliation on more equitable footing as *guests* and not hosts. Why is it that so many missional Christians seem so eager to start something of their own instead of joining with others already in the community doing good work?

Why is it that so many missional Christians seem so eager to start something of their own instead of joining with others already in the community doing good work?

I am not suggesting that this exact idea is something everyone should try, but I do find it interesting that despite the enormous diversity—ethnically, socioeconomically, and denominationally—of the many churches in my neighborhood, incoming groups rarely find ways to deeply root and connect with those who are different, despite their stated intentions to do exactly that. So perhaps the call to collaboration remains relevant for the very reason we assert its importance to begin with: communities are changed and transformed slowly and collaboratively—together in real partnership—and not by charismatic individuals or good ideas alone.

The Persistent Ghetto

Ultimately, as we pursue a parish ministry of place that practices listening locally, compassionate lament, and collaborative engagement, one geographic feature that must remain in focus is the reality, challenge, and universality of the *ghetto*. The persistence of ghettos in all of their various forms and signifiers—the hood, slums, *barrios*, *favelas*, skid row, the projects, and so forth—is simply a physical manifestation of social separation. Whether we identify these places as ethnic enclaves or the wrong side of the tracks, or even when people use *ghetto* as a pejorative colloquialism for "black," the fundamental reality of segregation is a phenomenon we've examined from urban Detroit to exurban South Dakota.

In mixing geographic metaphors, the important book *American Apartheid: Segregation and the Making of the Underclass* reminds us of the elusive public perception of segregation. "Most Americans vaguely realize that urban America is still a residentially segregated society, but few appreciate the depth of black segregation or the degree to which it is maintained by ongoing institutional arrangements and contemporary individual actions."[12] Like the South African state of "apart-ness" that so clearly divided colonial society into four racial groups (white, black, colored, and Indian), a similar arrangement persists in the United States, one that constructs and perpetuates the "other America,"[13] an invisible underclass that is largely isolated from the structures and opportunities of the dominant culture.

And while the particular details of some of these divisions are indeed uniquely American—highways, suburbs, housing, schools, and churches—there is also a curious universality to ghettos. No matter where people choose to settle and engage in place making, there's a sense in which we always gravitate toward locating our lives within specific boundaries and along color lines. However, as I've repeatedly emphasized in previous chapters, even though this tendency could be described as normal human behavior (sociological, evolutionary, etc.), the detrimental nature of homogeneous clustering that leads to the prevalence of ghettos is painfully underestimated.

Without an understanding of how deeply our cities are bound to the racial logic of exclusion and segregation, we simply cannot make a dent in the enormous momentum behind its persistence. The forward march of structural segregation largely overshadows our individual frustration or displeasure with the arrangement. For example, to use an economic metaphor, we may personally dislike the products or practices of powerful corporations (e.g., McDonald's or Walmart), but our individual actions to critique or even organize against such entrenched and well-resourced interests often seem small. Likewise, in the complexity that is the city, how can a Christian community, however big or small, make a dent in the racial logic and patterns of exclusion that create and enforce the universality of ghettos?

A Chinese Mustard Seed

The summer of my senior year at the University of Washington was full of transition and adventure, but much of my time and energy went into preparing for a "vision trip" to Central Asia. Our primary location was in the city of Urumqi, the largest city in the Xinjiang province of northwestern China. I was traveling with a relatively small team, and our host was a family of long-term missionaries in the city who had been working to build relationships with the Uyghur people, a predominantly Muslim ethnic minority group of Turkic descent who are scattered throughout Central Asia. Though my grandparents had immigrated from the coastal region of Toishan, a very different area, this was my first trip to the motherland, and I was eager to take it all in.

Looking back, I'd like to think we took our cultural preparation seriously in the months prior to travel, and for the most part we did the best we could with our time and resources. We were predominantly Chinese Americans with some basic language skills and cultural familiarity who would be teaching English in a vocational university setting and building relationships with students and other locals. While the trip went smoothly overall, with each passing year since that memorable summer, I am struck by a couple of nagging recognitions.

First, in spite of our good intentions and diligent training, nothing could have adequately prepared us for the challenging task of engaging with the Uyghur community in Urumqi in any meaningful way. Second, the reason we were so poorly prepared for this specific work was that we simply could not overcome the structural segregation that existed and persists today between the dominant Han Chinese and the marginalized Uyghurs whose lives were ghettoized, literally and figuratively, by Chinese policies that effectively kept the Uyghur people isolated, poor, and under the control of the state.

Like so many other cities, the dividing color lines in Urumqi are clear. Sociologist Blaine Kaltman describes how

> Ren Min Lu (People's Road) effectively divides Urumqi along a north-south axis. The north side is the city's Han section, and it is far more developed than the south side. Across Ren Min Lu, on Urumqi's south side is Er Dao Qiao Market, Urumqi's most famous Uighur market area . . . and the shabby brick ghetto that surrounds it.[14]

When speaking with my classroom of predominantly Han Chinese students about a planned excursion to the Uyghur market, I distinctly remember their casual but pointed remarks about Uyghur people.

“You shouldn’t go there,” they insisted in their limited English. “Uyghurs are bad people; they are criminals.” Others went on to suggest their biological inferiority. “Those people have poor morals because they are not smart.” At first, I was taken aback, but as I’ve come to reflect on their blatant racism, I realize that their fear and prejudice came from observable individual assumptions. Sadly, when our trip to the night market resulted in one of our team members getting knifed in an attempted mugging (thankfully, he recovered quickly), it only confirmed my students’ insistence of the Uyghurs’ inherent criminality and violent tendencies.

I’ve often thought about those awkward classroom exchanges with my young Chinese students and wondered what I would say now if I could go back to that time and place to do it over again. In the years since, I’ve watched with sadness as violent riots between Uyghurs and Han Chinese have erupted again and again in the streets of Urumqi, and I’ve seen the painful similarities between those streets on the other side of the world and the racial conflicts on my local neighborhood block that flare up every summer. Is it possible to imagine a place and a community beyond the reach of this universally downward spiral of exclusion, inequity, and violence?

Though the situation often looks bleak, and at times the lament seems to have no end, I’m reminded of Jesus’ simple metaphor of the mustard seed. It is a tiny little seed that seems insignificant, yet it grows into a tree to provide shelter and rest for the birds in the garden (Lk 13:18-19). As a sign of the kingdom of God, the mustard seed is a small seed of faith that in time takes root and transforms its environment. At first glance, it would seem that I have no miraculous stories to share from that summer in Urumqi; we did not single-handedly break down the walls of hostility between the Chinese and Uyghurs, and we certainly did not rescue anyone from a life of poverty and exclusion in the ghetto.

However, the dissonant nature of the overall experience, along with the troubling conversations and realities of urban segregation, has burrowed into my memory in a strangely formative way. The seed that was planted through my summer in China exposed my naivete about exclusion but also gave me hope for an alternative possibility of life together, whether in faraway places or just down the street. I still long for that possibility—for places thick with rooted communities and parishes that disrupt the fear and racial logic of the ghetto with creativity and incarnational imagination. Somehow, despite my occasional doubts as I read the news about our world both near and far, deep down I still believe that seeds of hope and faith, when nurtured by the life of God's kingdom, bear fruit for the *shalom* of the city.

- 6 -

Gentrification

"The valley is for poor people!"

I'll never forget the palpable sense of awkwardness and anger that filled the auditorium of the Rainier Valley Cultural Center that October night in 2006. A couple of hundred neighbors and residents of 98118, one of the most ethnically and socioeconomically diverse zip codes in the state of Washington and the nation, had gathered to hear from a city council task force about an "exciting time of growth and renewal" for our historic neighborhood. The awkwardness came from a part of the presentation when city officials proudly presented large and colorful illustrations of what the proposed new urban village could look like. They smiled and enthusiastically pointed out the midrise condos with gleaming walls of glass, and the convenient light rail station that would be built right at the intersection of Martin Luther King Jr. Way and Rainier Avenue South.

But instead of hearing the applause and excitement they expected, their elaborate diagrams and depictions of the new Rainier Valley were met with jeers and boos from the crowd. People yelled out from their seats—"we don't want that here!" and "where do *you* live?!"—as the city officials sheepishly attempted to backpedal from their confident presentation. And that's when I heard the rallying cry of the evening: "The Valley is for poor people!" A woman near the front had cried out in what seemed like a combination of exasperation and indignation, and her voice rose above the crowd. As soon as she spoke the words, the auditorium erupted in applause, her simple sentiment capturing the mood of the evening so succinctly.

As I witnessed the drama unfolding from my seat near the back of the auditorium, I felt torn. Like many of my neighbors, I was both amused and annoyed at the city planners who clearly did not have a good sense of who was in the audience and how they felt about their community. The blight and dilapidation some city officials spoke of so carelessly was seen as history and authenticity to many locals, even if it was a little rough around the edges. It may not have looked like much, but it was theirs, and the proposed "new and improved" Rainier Valley just seemed out of place. People were rightfully angry that the plans for development did not seem to include them in the process and understandably frustrated that yet again, promises of change would only benefit those who'd be able to afford the new, more expensive neighborhood.

However, I could also see how the well-intentioned developers and city planners were also frustrated by the process. They were doing their best to include affordable housing and incorporate public feedback through a citizens' review committee, but there was simply no way to please everyone. Costs for redevelopment were significant and would need to be offset by more income diversity in the area. The inevitable change of growth was on the horizon, but the financial and political pressures limited their development options. The Rainier Valley may have once been for poor people, but with all the money and momentum behind its so-called up-and-coming status, the changes seemed unstoppable. Wouldn't some development and investment, however imperfect, be better than no development at all?

The "G-Word"

We've all seen it happening—the trendy new café or bakery that opens in an old industrial warehouse, or the fashionable boutique behind a restored historic storefront. These new urban spaces attract customers and visitors who, for whatever reason, don't quite look like the longtime residents of the neighborhood. Gentrification—the process of redevelopment, transition, and the subsequent displacement of lower-income people that occurs in allegedly blighted neighborhoods—is a complex and controversial topic. Though its existence as a widespread urban phenomenon has been documented for several decades, growing research on the causes and effects of gentrification has become more prominent in the past ten to fifteen years, in part because of its increased visibility in cities all across the country.

For some, gentrification (the "g-word") has become an inflammatory topic because of all the tension and conflict it evokes, with its numerous connections to race, place, history, and power. Debates over class privilege, economic development, and cultural imperialism often leave people defensive, frustrated, and at odds with each other over who belongs where. For these reasons and many others, it seems to me that Christians face a unique opportunity to step into the challenging space of this complex urban topic with grace, humility, and all the postures of listening and collaboration we explored in the last chapter.

Christians face a unique opportunity to step into the challenging space of this complex urban topic with grace.

Gentrification has many faces and stories, and its outcomes cannot be easily condemned or celebrated in a singular fashion. Like many of the interrelated issues of race and place we've explored in the urban context, the signs and implications of communities in the process of change can be read and interpreted in a plurality of ways. As we look at this concept and its connections to historic and cultural injustices, I want us to recognize the boundaries and color lines of these communities in transition so that we can engage with our neighbors and work toward reconciliation.

The Allure of Urban "Cool"

To understand gentrification in a wider frame, we first have to take the powerful cultural and economic forces of "cool" into account. It's probably very *un*cool to use *cool* as a descriptor of whatever is "in": trendy, hip, hot, now, fashionable, or whatever denotes the shifting subjectivity of coolness. Regardless, for our purposes, cool is simply a signifier of what I'll describe as a particular *aesthetic experience* in the city. Cool is about an intangible look, vibe, or feeling that accompanies the experience of urban places, products, and cultural goods that embody the Zeitgeist of popular culture in the city.

To use a metaphor from hip-hop, a decent synonym for cool (for the moment, at least) is *swagger* (or *swag*). Defining swag is yet another semantic spiral, but even those of us not very familiar with (or fond of) hip-hop culture can recognize its inherent cool factor. Hip-hop *culture*, of course, is more than a musical genre or style. Just like classical, jazz, or punk, the musicality of rap or R & B is simply one part of a whole system of cultural knowledge and practices. For hip-hoppers, you can't parse and define swag; you simply recognize it, know it, and live it as it relates to authentic expression and experience. In the same way, it's difficult to define what makes something cool in the urban context, especially because of the cultural diversity that exists in the city. What's cool to one person may seem strange, artificial, or cliché to another.

With that said, the particular kind of urban cool we'll focus on in the context of gentrification is better illustrated—or dramatized—than explained. And in order to make sense of this example, I have to use one final ambiguous but important signifier in the city: the urban "hipster." Hipsters, however imprecise and undefinable the term, are a point of interest for the critical role they play in catalyzing gentrification. With roots and connotations in earlier concepts such as hippie or bohemian, the contemporary hipster (though highly resistant to categorical labels) is typically a young, white urbanite with a tenuous opposition to whatever is deemed mainstream. And while "hipsterism as an identifiable phenomenon very clearly has to do with particular fashions, and fashion micro-trends, which are notoriously hard to explain,"[1] the prevalence of hipsterism of various stripes is also quite obvious to many living in cities today. The widespread propagation and popularity of hipsterism is a confusing contradiction of its alternative and ironic aesthetics.

Perhaps the most effective or at least most popular dramatization of hipsters is enacted in the sketch-comedy television series *Portlandia,* which lampoons the subcultural habits of hipsters with layered satire and humor. The city of Portland is in many ways the perfect urban context to parody hipsters in their natural habitat: a young, predominantly white, and recently "cool" city, whose unofficial motto is to "keep Portland weird." Portland is the whitest major city in the United States, and its shifting urbanism is indicative of emerging patterns in other cities across the country. In this context, *Portlandia* tirelessly satirizes numerous hipster caricatures: the feminist bookstore owner, the organic vegan foodie, the broody indie musician, and the ubiquitous urban cyclist.

One of my favorite *Portlandia* sketches, titled "OVER," presents the ironic interdependence of what's cool—including fixed-gear bikes, shell art, and creatively styled beards. In the cyclical sequence of whatever is cool and then suddenly "over" because it has gone mainstream, urban consumers are stuck in the endless pursuit of an arbitrary, constructed aesthetic of urban cool. Cold-brew coffee and folk music may be fashionable today, but whatever trend becomes popular inevitably heads toward irrelevance, at least for hipsters, who must constantly be ahead of the curve in consuming obscure and unknown foods, music, and other artisanal cultural goods. This moving target of what's cool is an important concept to understand in the shifting urban landscape that serves as the backdrop for gentrification.

It is also worth noting, however briefly at this point, that hipsterism has obviously spilled over into contemporary Christianity as well, particularly among younger evangelicals, millennials, or whatever generational category one may use to characterize the demographic swell of those who are roughly eighteen to thirty-four. These masses of Christians whose savvy use of technology and social media is as natural as breathing are often accessorized by the same fashionable aesthetics that make *Portlandia* ironic. Cool Christianity is a piece of the gentrification conversation, but for now, let's return to the wider context of how cities are being reshaped by the perception, experience, and pursuit of a particularly cool lifestyle.

Fleeing the City

Fleeing or flight has taken many forms in the history of settlement space in general, and for cities, the basic reality that populations with shared interests or characteristics act in groups is as foundational as the social clustering I've repeatedly identified as the default logic of place. However, in the historical context of gentrification, there is an important distinction between fleeing *from* and fleeing *to.* The former is typically motivated by fear—of the other, the ghetto, or any other perceived threat to comfort, convenience, or safety. But the latter—fleeing *to*—is a different kind of flight and could also be described in terms of attraction. Fleeing *from* something is easily understood, but the reason I want to frame fleeing *to* as another form of flight as opposed to just movement or migration is that the process of gentrification is best understood in the context of mirrored flights, and the symbiosis or relatedness that has always existed between urban and suburban areas, and the populations who locate their lives there.

In chapter four, we explored how highways created a convenient and efficient way to move large populations outside the city for the creation of suburbia. In so doing, highways literally paved the way for flight and fleeing all the undesirable things about cities like congestion, pollution, and poverty. And because of the economic policies and structures that racialized suburbia, this kind of mass exodus from cities has often been labeled as *white flight*, the large-scale departure of whites from urban, inner-city areas. White flight made racial homogeneity and upward mobility possible in the neighborhoods, schools, and churches of suburbia, so of course the corollary reality for the urban areas left behind was an inverse image of that same homogeneity. Places labeled as the inner city were stigmatized with the social characteristics of poverty and crime in communities populated exclusively by people of color.

This classic urban-suburban divide is still a prominent feature of many US cities, and its resilience is rooted in the history of the ghettos created as a result of the resources extracted from the city in white flight. Fleeing citizens took their tax base, social capital, and direct investment with them, and very little was left behind. For example, as the post–World War II housing boom catalyzed suburban development across the country, the opposite kind of housing was being constructed near urban cores at the same time: government-subsidized public housing. But the critical difference between government subsidies in housing was the economic outcome: for suburban homes, government-backed loans provided the opportunity to gain the equity and wealth of homeownership, while government-subsidized public housing projects locked poor communities into a cycle of rent and dependency. For these reasons and many others we've already explored, white flight was extraordinarily costly to communities of color.

The patterns of fleeing were predictably consequential for the church as well. Urban pastor and theologian Eric Jacobsen describes the effects:

> For the past two decades . . . we have been abandoning our strategic locations within city cores and traditional neighborhoods, and we have tried to create for ourselves a new kind of society in the form of suburban megachurches. And as individual Christians, we have marched right along with the rest of our culture and moved our homes outside of the urban core into the sanitized world of the suburbs. Even when we have not participated directly in this radical shift, we have come to view the particularities of functioning in the midst of the city . . . as inconveniences rather than as opportunities for ministry. . . . Unfortunately, if we were to take a hard look at how Christians in this country have come to view their cities, we would have to conclude that our views have not necessarily been shaped by the Bible, prayer, or meaningful discussions among fellow Christians. It might be more accurate to say that the fear of cities, or the fear of one another, or possibly the love of convenience has been the actual basis of much of our current perceptions about the city.[2]

Though Jacobsen is more subtle about the racial logic of the church's steady flight to the suburbs, the utopian metaphor of a sanitized world is appropriate. Sheltered from the "dirtiness" of urban problems, predominantly white churches could distance themselves from the inconvenience and discomfort of ethnic and economic diversity in the city.

Return Flight

However, an interesting thing started happening as the children who were born and raised in the sanitized suburbs grew up. The somewhat bland and predictable big-box landscape of suburbia, which author James Howard Kunstler famously describes as "the geography of nowhere,"[3] began to look less appealing. Somehow the endless parking lots and strip malls, combined with growing commute times between business parks and McMansions, all seemed to contribute to a growing sense of uniformity and isolation in the formerly utopian suburbs. Perhaps homogeneity and upward mobility were less desirable in actuality, or the disappointment came from the typical angst and disillusionment that often accompanies a generational shift. Regardless of the source of the change, one thing was becoming clear: suburbia was no longer cool.

I realize this is a generalization, and certainly many people have held on to their dreams of suburban convenience and feel satisfied enough. But the distinct sense that the suburban culture and lifestyle was being displaced by new forms of popular urbanism in the 1990s and 2000s is nevertheless an important cultural shift to recognize. This shift occurred on many fronts, from the explosive popularity of hip-hop (an urban art form whose primary consumer was young, white, suburban males) to the critiques of suburbia in movies like *Pleasantville*, a 1998 film with humorous satire about the cultural restraints of suburban life. Even the enormously popular and influential television sitcom *Friends* (1994–2004) is representative of a kind of urban lifestyle, with its Manhattan setting and cast of young, single professionals. Consider the contrast between a traditional suburban sitcom like *Family Ties* (1982–1989) and the in-city living of *Friends,* whose characters' social lives converged not in the living room of a nuclear family but instead around the public seating of Central Perk, a fictional coffee house in New York's Greenwich Village.

As these cultural markers signaled a renewed interest in urbanism, so were cities themselves remaking their urban cores to attract a new generation of professionals, consumers, and trendsetters. With the recognition that growing suburban sprawl was in many ways economically and environmentally unsustainable, planners and city officials began to look toward higher-density development on underutilized land. Throughout the 1990s, downtown areas across the country were transformed from inner-city ghettos and industrial warehouses into central business districts and new commercial spaces for retail, entertainment, and commerce. Massive public and private investment built high-rise condominiums, sports stadiums, and transit infrastructure to accommodate growth, and people flocked to these remade cities to fulfill their new urban dreams.

However, there was one big problem in the midst of all this construction and redevelopment: people were already living in these allegedly underused and blighted places. Many had put down roots for entire generations and took offense at the notion that the places where they had located their lives were seen as run-down and ready for a wrecking ball. How would you feel if someone walked into your living room with an expression of disgust and assumed you'd be eager to have your home demolished?

How would you feel if someone walked into your living room with an expression of disgust and assumed you'd be eager to have your home demolished?

Whole communities of people (almost always communities of color), who for decades had been abandoned by white flight and public neglect, were suddenly in the crosshairs of the many economic opportunists who saw the dollar signs in the dirt. These ethnic enclaves, housing projects, and former ghettos were now occupying some of the most valuable land in the city because of their proximity to the new urban amenities that were transforming downtown landscapes into places for both the *nouveau riche* and the many other young urbanites who aspired to be like them. So what would become of their newly desirable land? Would these "indigenous" urban dwellers be fairly compensated for their prime real estate?

Waves of suburban transplants, eager to settle into a new urban lifestyle, were remaking the city once again. Just as their parents' generation had fled the city to create suburbia, they were now fleeing from their distaste for the blandness of Pleasantville. Life in the new city just seemed too attractive to pass up, and like the explorers and settlers long before their time, their plan to embark on an urban adventure would in time prove to be costly for the native inhabitants of the lands they would "discover" in the city. In short, this was a return flight to the city, a departure from the boring suburbs to the much cooler urban places being constructed in historic and colorful neighborhoods. What happens when the former ghetto is labeled as an up-and-coming community?

Gentrification in Action

For those who live at the whim of others with the resources to remake the city as they see fit, there's an old familiarity with the patterns of race and place that lead to cycles of development, transition, and displacement. The structures of exclusion that make gentrification possible are rooted in power and economic disparity, and the sense of powerlessness and resignation that many of the displaced feel is a perpetual reminder that they live at the bottom of an urban hierarchy.

It starts small and seems harmless at first—since no one was using that old, abandoned building, it seems like some new development a good thing. But the incremental changes that occur on the surface of the built environment of a neighborhood in transition are like the tip of an iceberg. Below the surface of what seems like superficial change is an enormous block of investment resources, shifting cultural values, and economic momentum. Underneath the façade of that newly renovated café, natural grocer, or trendy boutique is often a particular history and community whose collective stories are being overwritten by the process of redevelopment that has all the subtlety of a steamroller.

It's true that some degree of change and growth is inevitable in every urban community, and the transitions are always difficult for some. But what makes gentrification especially dangerous is both the naive assumption of overall neighborhood improvement and the invisibility of those at the margins of change. It probably shouldn't surprise me anymore, but I am continually struck by the things that some people in my neighborhood say, often with no recognition of how they sound or what their casual musings assume.

"Why would anyone *not* buy organic produce?!"

"Who would send their own child to that school?!"

"I'm *so* glad that _____ (house, building, group, landmark) is gone! It was such a _____ (nuisance, eyesore, problem)!"

And conversely:

"I'm *so* glad that new _____ (store, restaurant, event) is here now! It's going to make this place just like _____ (that other desirable neighborhood that's no longer affordable)!"

Perhaps these are just moments of honesty expressed in passing, but the many assumptions behind their brief sentiments reflect the stark racial and socioeconomic isolation that occurs in gentrifying neighborhoods. Simply put, the more we locate our lives in pockets of cultural familiarity, the more difficult it becomes to imagine the desires, values, and habits of others. Familiarity becomes dangerously normal, and this bias, coupled with a naive, individualistic presumption of the neutrality of place, is what drives the cultural tension in gentrification.

If I generally assume that (1) my consumer choices are right, sensible, and good, and (2) there's a basic equality of opportunity, resources, and geographic choice in my neighborhood, then why wouldn't someone want to buy organic produce, send their kids to good schools, and shop at nice stores while walking down safe streets? Of course gentrification seems like a good thing to those who benefit from the changes and see them as normal and desirable!

I don't think my neighbors are naive about the *existence* of poverty, but I do believe they are often in the dark when it comes to imagining and understanding poverty as a way of life, especially among poor communities of color that are culturally isolated. John Hayes, the founder of InnerCHANGE, a Christian order among the poor, offers this simple reminder: "Poverty, we know about. It's poor *people* we do not know."[4] Those at the bottom of the urban hierarchy are sadly invisible to many of us because "they exist in our spiritual blind spot. Too late, their images register in our rearview mirror of guilt."[5]

Additionally, today's urban poverty is frequently masked or hidden. Thousands upon thousands of families in urban America are hovering just above the poverty line, hanging on by a thread. The tiniest of unanticipated expenses can send these families right into the downward spiral of housing and food insecurity, but many work hard to hide the indignities and shame of being seen as poor in America. Our default cultural avoidance of the poor is precisely the reason Christians should be paying more attention to their lives instead of justifying our general apathy or offering some charitable sympathy out of guilt.

When a shiny new (or carefully restored) building goes up in an older urban neighborhood and the opening business draws a crowd, ribbons are cut and progress is celebrated. But we rarely pause to consider the entire cost of that development. Who is on the underside or outside of the transactions that resulted in this structural change in the community? Whose values or interests were cut short or cast aside in the excavation of the land? Sometimes, it's not only old buildings that are demolished in the process of "revitalization." Far too many hopes and dreams have been lost in the wreckage of the old hood. Perhaps the greatest cost of gentrification is the inevitable erasure of communities and histories that occurs through transition and displacement.

Whether quickly or gradually, gentrification ensures that direct investment will cause the overall cost of living in an area to increase. Rental housing, property taxes, and essential consumer goods and services all go up in price as the landscape shifts underneath the feet of new residents and businesses. For reasons that I hope are now obvious, a neighborhood quickly becoming more expensive is not a "rising tide that lifts all boats." Those who can afford to stay may benefit, but the front lines of the displaced are always the most vulnerable: transients, immigrants, resettled refugees, the elderly or disabled, and the working poor. Living on the margins of change means that even

Perhaps the greatest cost of gentrification is the inevitable erasure of communities and histories that occurs through transition and displacement.

the slightest increases in living costs can push an individual or family into precarious circumstances.

Unfortunately, much of the displacement that occurs in gentrifying areas is largely invisible to those who are often too busy enjoying their new urban lifestyles to notice. When businesses or people come and go, we naturally presume it is someone else's issue if it doesn't affect us directly. If I could sum up the combinations of ignorance and apathy I've heard over the years related to gentrification, it would be something along the lines of "places always change, and that's just the way it goes." When we remain in the default perspective of geographic neutrality, the changes around us seem little more than incidental and inevitable.

But I hope we can begin to recognize that gentrification and its many hidden costs is not an urban inevitability that we must sit back and accept. I believe that Christians can and must see things differently, and that the nature of *placed* discipleship calls the church into a unique tension of informed advocacy *with* the poor in the many urban neighborhoods that are experiencing the painful transitions of gentrification.

Grace Flows Like Water

A repeated, foundational idea of this book—that place matters in God's economy and therefore the Christian life—has already been articulated in a variety of ways, but one of my favorite theology and geography metaphors comes from the book *Geography of Grace*, which says "grace is like water—it flows downhill and pools up in the lowest places."[6] As I've reflected on the Christian story throughout my life—in Scripture, history, and embodied in my experiences of people and places—I've come to see that the gifts of God's gracious love have a tangible, physical trajectory. Again and again, I've seen how embodied grace gravitates toward the unlikely and unseen places underneath the worldly preoccupations we have with wealth and power.

My sense of wonder at God's grace, which streams freely into the lowest, hardest places, is deepened by the mysterious logic of lavish, divine gifts flowing into the gutters and valleys of pain, poverty, and loss. Why would the infinitely good and powerful God choose to take on lowly human form and be born into helplessness and poverty? The self-emptying downward mobility of the incarnation is the truest picture we have of humanity submitted to God's will, and it continues to shape the character of God's mission in this broken world.

Cities exhibit all the triumphs and tragic failures of human civilization, and as we've seen, gentrification is but one piece of a larger puzzle in trying to make urban communities flourish for all and not just the few. In every city, Christians are strategically located—vocationally, residentially, socially—to bear witness to the city of God, a place of peace and healing that evokes all the shalom of the new Jerusalem. How can the church harness the creative vision of that heavenly place—where God's kingdom breaks into our present reality—for the good of the neighborhood?

If we follow the geography of grace in cities, then one place I believe we'll find ourselves is not primarily with the "movers and shakers" above us, but "underneath the bridge with the moved and shaken."[7] However, I want to be clear: this does not mean that somehow in God's economy the powerful and privileged are inherently blissful, condemned, or undeserving of grace. The false dichotomy of God's preferential option for the poor presumes that CEOs and celebrities are forsaken in favor of the destitute and vulnerable, but I believe this is an unnecessary and divisive construal of God's great concern for those who find themselves at the bottom of society. Rather than suggesting we should pit stratified groups against one another, I see it another way: the deep reservoirs of God's grace we discover among the poor draw *all* people—privileged *and* powerless—to the mystery, beauty, and surprising reversal of God's kingdom.

And so we hold up the plight of the poor and disenfranchised and focus our attention there in order to better understand where God is moving from below and how it demands our faithful stewardship, whether we have many resources or very few. Regardless of what we have, this geography of grace in the city takes us right into the uncomfortable "Samarias" we identified in chapter two: the places we've been conditioned to avoid for fear of difference and cultural conflict. If we're going to engage gentrification constructively and Christianly, then we'll have to cross over the boundaries of race and class into that difficult space of being in-between.

Tensions and Tipping Points

At the beginning of this chapter, I described the tension I felt being caught between angry neighbors and frustrated developers in my immediate community. In no way is this an easily resolvable tension, though at times I wish it were. I wish I could provide three steps to solving the gentrification puzzle so that everyone could win; longtime residents could feel honored, affordability and history could be preserved, diversity and equity could be upheld, *and* new development could bring change that's widely embraced. Unfortunately, cities and neighborhoods just don't work that way, and we're often left with the balancing act of trying to minimize certain risks and costs while at the same time compromising toward hopeful but uncertain change.

Yet once again, this is where I believe Christians can be strategically positioned in places of tension to offer both simple gestures of peacemaking and deeper practices of reconciliation.

In particular, I want to loosely borrow Malcolm Gladwell's idea of "tipping points" as a way to frame neighborly Christian engagement in gentrifying communities.[8] As we've seen, gentrification is a complex process that occurs on many fronts, but I believe Christians can intentionally and collectively place themselves at unique boundaries to cross unspoken color lines in ways that tip the scales toward justice and belonging.

These few suggestions are hardly comprehensive, but I think they get at the heart of the matter by reshaping the social fabric of communities in a more hospitable direction. In gentrifying neighborhoods, thoughtful Christians can participate in "little things [that] can make a big difference"[9] by rejecting the allure of cool, disrupting the momentum of profitability, and joining with the stranger in both celebration and lament.

Cooling Off

Certain enclaves in the city of Portland—"weird" as they may seem, with unique and artsy eccentricities—would, in my opinion, do well to pay closer attention to the irony of being driven by the (il)logic of hipsterism. For all the attempts at rejection of the mainstream, Portland, and many places like it, has in fact further popularized a superficial aesthetic of cool. Hipsterism is essentially trapped in a perpetual state of exclusion; that which is deemed uncool is to be rejected in favor of the shifting markers of whatever is trending. For many caught up in the aesthetics of cool, it's a hamster wheel of consumer accessorizing, but the costs of that consumption are paid for by their neighbors on the margins.

Alberta Street in northeast Portland was once the heart of the small but historic African American community in the city. Black families had been redlined and restricted to that area, but they put down roots and made it their own. Yet in patterns mirrored across many US cities, the past decade has seen a steady influx of new businesses and residents who represent all the trending demographics of the city: young, white, and some combination of affluent and artistic sensibilities. Today, the Alberta Arts District is a highly gentrified neighborhood representative of a city-wide shift from 2000 to 2010. In 2011, *The Oregonian* reported how "the city core didn't become whiter simply because lots of white residents moved in, the data shows. Nearly 10,000 people of color, mostly African Americans, also moved out. And those who left didn't move to nicer areas."[10] The cool factor of Alberta's trendy boutiques and restaurants is undeniable, and the transition that occurred there should at least catch the local church's attention.

The church's general capitulation (i.e., "cultural captivity," in the language of Soong-Chan Rah, John Perkins, and many others) to societal trends such as consumer aesthetics and social behavior is nothing new, but the return flight to the city has had enormous negative consequences that must be examined more closely. And just as Eric Jacobsen identified urban flight as a problematic trend for suburban churches, so has gentrification—driven by the aesthetics and economics of cool—become the latest troubling result of groupthink.

Amid the rapid propagation of cool Christianity through the cultural apparatus of technology (take Instagram, for example), I've come to believe that slicker marketing and so-called innovations in the church have largely failed to examine their assumptions about the appeal of cool. In the pursuit of very particular aesthetics—from design fonts to video editing—cool Christians are finding themselves caught in hipsterism's perpetual state of exclusion through adopting brand identities that implicitly create hierarchy and reject difference. The social and racial logic of cool, which contains various forms of cultural homogeneity, has been consumed instead of questioned.

Rejecting the allure of cool does not mean the creation of a legalistic catalog of acceptable consumer items or practices, but it should at the very least encourage a closer and more honest interrogation of our attraction to said consumer goods and experiences. For example, in what ways have the creative authorities of cool co-opted our aesthetic sensibilities and convinced us that uniquely artisan and organic lifestyles should be pursued by everyone? I'd like to simply suggest that the innate and deep-seated desire to be seen—and to see ourselves—as cool is one of the dangerous distractions at the root of social division. Most of us who can recall adolescence should remember how powerfully this force orders our world and fractures our society.

Life together as Christians simply cannot function under the authoritarian demands of cool. Communities of color have repeatedly paid the price for occupying the unenviable position of living at the shifting margins of the city, and those of us with the resources to make geographic decisions based on consumer aesthetics (however cool or uncool we may see them) should take notice. What might happen if churches saw the transitions of gentrification as socioeconomically significant and not just the result of lifestyle choices? Imagine an urban community where cool Christians followed the plight of the poor instead of the latest stylistic trends! While it's true that some forms of urban ministry have arguably become cool for some, once the exoticism of poverty wears off, there's very little that's cool about the slow and difficult ministry of working incarnationally against structural injustice in the city.

Life together as Christians simply cannot function under the authoritarian demands of cool.

Prophets Against Profits

Of the many forces at work in gentrifying neighborhoods, few are as significant and difficult to counteract as the momentum of profitability. Once the opportunities for profitable investment are identified, the magical capital of free markets tends to snowball on the promises of big returns. Gentrification attracts those who stand to gain great wealth in the large-scale transition of an entire community, and for Christians, I believe this powerfully attractive force requires a prophetic intervention in order to "let justice roll down like waters" (Amos 5:24) as deep and rushing as the revenue streams that flow to real-estate developers and investors.

While profitability is an essential economic reality in general, profits earned through gentrification often come at the expense of those at the bottom, who are displaced by more affluent neighbors. In my own community, I've seen examples of apartment rental rates and the cost of staple consumer items nearly doubling in a matter of months, and it begs the question—how much profit is enough? Is there such a thing as a *reasonable* and *just* profit instead of a perpetually maximized profit? These are difficult conversations for the many Christians who have been culturally conditioned to revere the growth potential of free markets without question, but when places built on a history of racial exclusion profit on a continuation of those patterns, then faithful discipleship must call the church to imagine viable prophetic alternatives.

Old Testament scholar Walter Brueggemann reminds us that the primary mode of prophetic engagement is not only angry protest, but it is the balance of "criticizing and energizing" communities around a common cause that activates prophetic ministry.[11] Something as simple as supporting immigrant businesses, which are often outside the cool category in gentrifying neighborhoods, can be a powerful and prophetic corrective to the tendency to replace locally owned small businesses with higher-end retailers and their larger profitability. Immigrants are typically among the most productive grassroots entrepreneurs in neighborhood economies. Likewise, advocacy for work-force and affordable housing, accessible and livable wages, cooperative land trusts, and truly representative community leadership at the local level can each play a creative role in energizing and organizing vulnerable populations in the face of corporate interests with deep pockets and an appetite for profitability.

Last, I want to be clear: the *generation* of profit is not the problem or the enemy. In fact, profitability of various types is essential for every economically sustainable neighborhood. Rather, it is the scale and *maldistribution* of profit in gentrification that preys on the vulnerable that must be questioned. All the current research on gentrification demonstrates that it "ultimately hits hardest at the least advantaged and most economically vulnerable."[12] What can be done to more equitably distribute not only the profits at the end of the equation but also the opportunity to earn profit or capital in the middle of the process? Redistribution at its best is not about moving around the dollars after the fact; it *is* about creating more access to a larger, more diverse constituency of workers who can generate wealth for themselves.

For example, the housing industry is very profitable in gentrifying areas because real estate developers can capitalize on the higher profit margins of products marketed to high-income earners (e.g., luxury condominiums or townhomes). Equitable redistribution of these profits may look like simply taxing of private developers' profits to build low-income rental housing. However, a more creative way to work toward profitability for all would be to truly incentivize developers to broaden their customer base to include a wider range of incomes to join in the equity building and wealth generation of ownership. The affordable housing crises in many of our cities will not be solved by tossing the crumbs of big real estate profits in the general direction of working-class families or individuals. Rather, we need a groundswell of community-based housing models such as land trusts, cooperatives, and cohousing that disrupt the traditional economics of private builders and investors. What if Christians with a unique perspective on the benefits of a shared economy (as we see throughout the book of Acts) could lead the way toward reimagining new forms of affordable housing for all?

Ultimately, some degree of gentrification will always exist in neighborhoods that change, but if the worst outcomes can be mitigated by more creative and prophetic means, then I believe the opportunity for the church to stand with those at the bottom could reveal deep wells of God's grace in surprising places. These reservoirs of reconciled neighbors may have untapped potential to offer the transformative, living waters of mercy and compassion in the city.

Your People Are My People

Of the many biblical examples we have of crosscultural belonging, few are as compelling as Ruth's loving declaration to her mother-in-law, Naomi: "Where you go I will go, and where you stay I will stay. Your people will be my people and your God my God" (Ruth 1:16). This remarkable story of joining with a cultural other is rightfully woven into the genealogy of Jesus, whose life was marked by all the same surprising transgressions of racial logic and cultural order that defined his day and age. What could the church accomplish if people experiencing generational urban poverty were not simply "the poor" in the abstract but *our* people? Simply identifying with those at the bottom of the societal ladder as *your people* is an urgent incarnational challenge for the parish church in the city.

Christians in gentrifying neighborhoods have the opportunity to join with others in simple and radical acts of hospitality that defy the expectations of coolness and profitability at the root of gentrification. These acts of celebration, solidarity, and lament take on many forms: the community potluck, the gardening cooperative, local organizing efforts, and casual neighborly encounters of both joy and grief. There are no simple solutions to the costly transitions that displace our vulnerable neighbors, but honest conversations and persistent crosscultural friendships can make thoughtful political action a people-centric cause and not just an issue-driven agenda. Together, these practices can have a meaningful effect on the delicate balance of preservation and development facing many urban communities that are living in the tension of gentrification.

My friend and neighbor John Helmiere, a Methodist church planter and social agitator with a unique perspective on collaborative community engagement, has spent the last few years organizing, cultivating, and constructing a remarkable street-corner space called the Hillman City Collaboratory, an incubator for social change. But for all the ways he and others have created a new, innovative, and entrepreneurial place for community, the key ingredients have been more classically simple: listening, hospitality, and liberation for the common good of the neighborhood. John has simply cultivated friendships across traditional boundaries and joined in true partnership

Honest conversations and persistent crosscultural friendships can make thoughtful political action a people-centric cause and not just an issue-driven agenda.

with the good folks who are making ends meet and looking for a place to call their own. Together, they are dreaming about the possibilities of what is birthed in our shared gardening, cooking, music making, and laughter around the table.

Looking back at that night in the Rainier Valley Cultural Center ten years ago, I wish I would have made more of an effort to really join my neighbors in those awkward spaces of race and place that are still at work in the ongoing changes in my neighborhood. Indeed, though the past decade of my work in the community has involved plenty of tough conversations, cross-cultural friendships, and the occasional protest, I think my efforts have fallen short more often than they've hit the mark. I've too frequently been sidelined by my own discomfort, my desires for convenience and efficiency, and the limitations of time and energy that plague us all.

With that said, I'm still hopeful. I see in Ruth's embrace of Naomi a moving story of belonging and reconciliation that reshaped a family into an unexpected but beautiful community. This strange new family being remade by the Spirit of God may be the key to the flourishing of the church and the urban neighborhoods where God's mission is inviting those in the city to belong to one another.

PART III

COMMUNITIES of BELONGING

A Strange Family

→

\- 7 -

Reconciliation

A Beautiful and Disruptive Story

Years of teaching in a university setting have taught me a few things about how people learn. Though I'm very much a work in progress when it comes to the art of teaching, one thing I'm always reminded of when I grade papers, read course evaluations, or meet with students during office hours is that some of their most lasting lessons learned are different from what I assumed I was teaching. What I've noticed is that their important takeaways are rarely just regurgitations of specific course content of terms, concepts, or obscure academic theories. Rather, the things students most often describe as they reflect on their overall learning are a result of impressions and subtleties in between the lines of the texts and lectures—tone, posture, emotion, and connection. Students seem to gravitate toward the personal stories, improvised moments of honest dialogue, and humorous anecdotes about my own struggles or ponderings.

These deeper takeaways are not totally unrelated to the course content, but they seem to surpass the technicality of terminology and point to a more holistic and empathic way of knowing and engaging. It seems to me that Christian reconciliation, however it is learned, is better served by this kind of deeper learning than by the technical and academic definitions of the concept alone. It is not that the academic work is unimportant; it is rather that the conceptual learning must work in conjunction with the practical, relational, and experiential aspects of reconciliation as a *lived theology*, not just a textbook theory.

As always, this is of course much easier said than done. Hungarian chemist-turned-philosopher Michael Polanyi (1891–1976) called one aspect of this kind of learning "tacit knowing." In his famous work *Personal Knowledge*, Polanyi describes how the modern technologies of science, computing, and engineering are unable "to reproduce a single violin of the kind the half-literate Stradivarius turned out as a matter of routine more than 200 years ago."[1] What did this seventeenth-century family know about wood, strings, and craftsmanship that modern technology has been unable to recreate? Polanyi suggests that the deep traditions of transformative apprenticeship cannot be taught by technical knowledge alone. In the same way, Christian reconciliation is tied to the deep traditions and practices of discipleship, and all of the communal, creative, and holistic ways of learning that come on the path of following Jesus with others.

You may not aspire to be the Stradivarius of reconciliation, but I believe stories—more specifically, the kinds of dynamic and interactive narratives that weave together the Christian story with our own stories—are one of the most effective ways to learn deeply about how reconciliation works and how it must be practiced in community. Stories provoke our imaginations and stir our ability to think creatively about humanity, divinity, and possibility. The Christian Scriptures are not a fixed literary artifact to parse and examine with cold, scientific precision, as if we were conducting a theological autopsy of sorts. Quite to the contrary, as Christians read Scripture through the eyes of faith and with the people of God, the text comes to life by drawing us into its stories to find the triune God revealed there, as well as our own identities caught up in the drama of God reconciling all things.

Of the many themes and ideas at work in this richly layered story, we'll focus on a simple notion that has preoccupied my reflections about reconciliation for several years now: that somehow, the church is "a place where God is forming a family out of strangers."[2] I'm borrowing this phrase from Stanley Hauerwas and William Willimon's book *Resident Aliens*, which explores perennial questions about the social dimensions of the church in contemporary society. For what and for whom is the church called together? What is the nature and character of Christian community in the world? Hauerwas and Willimon address these questions:

> The most creative social strategy we have to offer is the church. Here we show the world a manner of life the world can never achieve through social coercion or governmental action. We serve the world by showing it something that it is not, namely, a place where God is forming a family out of strangers. . . . The gospel begins with the pledge that, if we offer ourselves to a truthful story and the community formed by listening to and enacting that story in the church, we will be transformed into people more significant than we could ever have been on our own. As Barth says, "[The Church] exists . . . to set up in the world a new sign which is radically dissimilar to [the world's] own manner and which contradicts it in a way which is full of promise" (Church Dogmatics, 4.3.2.).[3]

There are numerous things going on in this dense excerpt, but I want to highlight two points of emphasis for our purposes. First, the social strategy of the church is not innovative, elaborate, or even strategic as we traditionally think of the word. There is no twelve-step, three-phase plan, no animated PowerPoint slideshow, and no eye-catching visual diagram to speak of. While those kinds of tools can certainly be useful, at the root level, the church—the gathering of people covenanted to God and one another—*is* the strategy. The communal life, witness, and fellowship of the church is the strategy, and it is characterized by a strange occurrence indeed: a place where socially estranged people are becoming family to each other.

The second point of emphasis is that the cause of this odd social arrangement is a story about good news. Once again, it's not a story whose static description of events is to be read or told at arm's length; rather, the very nature of the living story is a dynamic and invitational narrative that draws its participants into a place and a community defined by the story. The gospel is a truly transformative story that calls the people of God to offer themselves to the story in order to become something new and hopeful: a "contrast community" that points beyond itself to the Author of the story. What is the church except a people who embody and enact a story that comes to life as we imagine and reimagine its meaning for ourselves and our neighbors? The church inhabits a story that reframes belonging in a society of exclusion. And if we're living into the story rightly, then people who have every reason to be estranged from one another somehow find that they are becoming sisters, brothers, mothers, uncles, and

The gospel is a truly transformative story that calls the people of God to offer themselves to the story in order to become something new and hopeful: a "contrast community" that points beyond itself to the Author of the story.

cousins. Both the context and the content of this story are essential to understanding the community that forms around a reconciled and reconciling people.

A Strange Family

I'm pretty sure that most of us consider at least *someone* in our immediate or extended family a bit odd. Maybe you have a slightly quirky sibling, a strange cousin, or a peculiar grandparent. On some occasions, perhaps you'd rather not associate with them, but at the end of the day, they remain family, and hopefully some semblance of loyalty or obligation comes with that. We don't choose the family we're born into, but the bonds of blood should run deep, even when we disagree or experience the recurring conflict that comes with all families on some level. Ties of kinship necessitate patience and perseverance—even when we think someone is a little weird.

The common thread in these family ties is essentially about shared biology/genealogy and the shared sense of identity that develops in a particular family's history and relationships. For most of human history, the biological family has been the basic building block of society, the common denominator in the assumed social order. The specific boundaries and composition of the family have varied, of course, but the basic assumptions have remained largely the same: kinship by blood or marriage is an essential bond and a foundational context for understanding love, identity, and belonging.

But what happens when families are formed outside these traditional family structures? In contrast to the more dominant family model, there have always been alternative kinds of families whose boundaries and composition have transgressed the typical ties of blood, ethnicity, and lineage. Some cultural anthropologists call this phenomenon "fictive kinship," an arrangement by which families are formed in spite of bloodlines, and relationships of intimacy can bridge or cross perceived social divides. For example, the practice of adoption is one of the most common examples of fictive kinship. When someone is truly adopted into a new family, they are treated as if their belonging is as natural as being born into the family biologically. In some cases, the fictive nature of this kinship can even intensify the bonds of intimacy because of the depth of commitment required to truly become family in the face of cultural norms that prioritize traditional kinship.

Accordingly, there are many theological reasons that adoption is one of the primary metaphors for the apostle Paul's description of the composition of the church and how Gentile outsiders have been incorporated or grafted into Israel's story. Christians have become heirs of God's promises made to Abraham (Gen 12:2-3) precisely because we have been adopted into a new family with Christ as the foundation and head. Additionally, Jesus himself repeatedly reframes traditional notions of family throughout the Gospels as he describes new rules for fictive kinship and new ways to imagine family loyalty. For example, he insists that "whoever does God's will is my brother and sister and mother" (Mk 3:35). Even more controversially, in another instance, Jesus says, "If anyone comes to me and does not hate father and mother, wife and children, brothers and sisters—yes, even their own life—such a person cannot be my disciple" (Lk 14:26). What kind of strange family is this?

Jesus' common refrain of identifying his followers as sisters and brothers was neither a blatant condemnation of traditional kinship nor a casual nickname for his friends and supporters. Rather, this consistent effort to employ traditional familial language in nontraditional ways was part of a larger agenda: to form a particular and peculiar people whose sense of belonging and loyalty to one another surpassed the bonds of blood alone. The community shaped by this new kind of belonging would become convinced that the cultural boundaries of ethnicity and lineage, and even other boundaries such as socioeconomic status, were being redrawn or even removed by the radical acts of love and service embodied by Jesus' life and ministry.

It should not be surprising, then, that as Paul's pastoral work with the early church is thrown into cultural controversy due to questions of Jewish social practices and ethnic markers of identity in the face of Gentile outsiders, Paul is quick to remind his fledgling congregations that they are indeed "one household" in Christ, a family whose newly shared identity has to trump their notions of racial fidelity.

Beloved Community at Rainier Avenue Church

As we consider the strangeness of this new family, and the context and content of their stories of belonging, what are some contemporary parallels to this creative reframing? How are churches today drawing on this same story to become family in unusual ways and places?

In *Welcoming Justice,* Charles Marsh and John Perkins reflect on the role of the church in the unfinished business of the civil rights movement through Martin Luther King Jr.'s vision of "the beloved community," a community marked by peace and wholeness in spite of the racial violence and strife that divided the nation. In a metaphor that parallels strangers becoming family, people becoming a beloved community were moving out of estrangement toward a vision of reconciliation. Perkins, a living civil rights legend in his own right, asks, "What does it take to make beloved community happen? I really believe that it begins with a place. . . . If the church is going to offer some real good news in broken communities, it has to be committed to a place."[4]

Rainier Avenue Church (RAC), appropriately named for its specific urban location, has been proudly situated at the same intersection on Rainier Avenue South in Seattle's Rainier Valley for over one hundred years. Naturally, over the course of the last century, there have been a lot of changes in the neighborhood surrounding the church. Through various waves of growth and struggle, the relatively inconspicuous building and its congregation have experienced several challenging seasons as the community around it shifted, leaving people wondering whether they should seek out greener pastures. Most notably, from the late 1960s to early 1970s, an economic slump in Seattle was compounded by changing demographics in the neighborhood when racially restrictive housing policies were lifted due to fair-housing legislation.

With new people from different backgrounds moving into the area—African Americans, Asian immigrants, and other populations looking for affordable housing—some people expressed the common concerns that always accompany neighborhood change. Predictably, fearful cries of "not in my backyard" and "there goes the neighborhood" are powerful motivators for those with the resources and opportunity to move elsewhere. On top of it all, by the late 1970s, after the Vietnam War, waves of Southeast Asian refugees were being resettled in southeast Seattle, which added another layer of diversity to the ever-changing Rainier Valley.

Between the economic pressures to move and the social fears that catalyze white flight, people both inside the church and in the surrounding community fled en masse in what would later be seen as one of the most significant transitions the neighborhood had undergone in a whole generation. Some members of Rainier Avenue Church had already departed, and others were on their way out or considering a move. Even the denominational leadership was in discussion about a closure or relocation of the church in the midst of this difficult transition.

Thankfully, in what has now become an integral part of RAC's history and identity, a small but faithful group of older, white members—most of whom were longtime residents of the neighborhood—simply did not believe that closing their doors or moving away was the right thing to do. A handful of families who seemed to be taking the multiple community transitions in stride prayerfully wanted to remain committed to the place and the mission of the church, even if it meant weathering more hardship and change. By God's grace, their resilience and resolve in time proved to be an essential step of faith for RAC.

Not long after these few families had decided they weren't going anywhere, World Relief, a refugee resettlement organization that partners with local churches, invited RAC to consider sponsoring a refugee family from Laos. Though no one in the church had any experience with hosting refugees, and their exposure to Southeast Asian culture was minimal at best, once again their faithful willingness to serve was a key turning point in shaping RAC's culture of hospitality.

Soon after this initial family was settled, other Laotian families began attending the church, and in time their children grew up in the church and took on positions of leadership. To this day, there is a vibrant mix of Southeast Asian immigrants and second-generation Asian Americans residing in southeast Seattle and actively contributing to RAC. In addition to this cultural mix reflecting the diversity of the neighborhood, the relationships formed over time have resulted in global and local partnerships in community development, church planting, and the kind of foundational friendship that comes with a big, extended family.

As I consider why and how RAC has become a place where God is forming a family out of strangers, the ties of fictive kinship move in many directions. Even this brief look at one particular series of events is only a small slice of how the church has cultivated a unique way of practicing reconciliation and love of neighbor. Among other things, hospitality is always an essential ingredient, and I see it in action every week, from the Southeast Asian "aunties" serving tea during fellowship times to the volunteers who work with the many residents of Center Park, a nearby housing community for people with physical or mental disabilities and their caretakers. On midweek community nights, we welcome neighbors, students, and church folks to share a meal together, after which an occasionally unpredictable mix of cooking, tutoring, and mingling keeps the fellowship hall buzzing with activity.

But before I paint an idyllic picture of this diversity, it's also important to recognize that the day-to-day messiness of strangers becoming family is not always as easy as it sounds on paper. It would be inaccurate to portray this beautiful extended family as a noble and simple task made possible by everyone just mustering enough kindness to be extra thoughtful and nice to each other. Quite to the contrary, although the process of reconciliation certainly bears unique and transformative fruit in a community, its cultivation is often slow, laborious, and fraught with the thorns and thistles of discomfort and uncertainty.

Although the process of reconciliation certainly bears unique and transformative fruit in a community, its cultivation is often slow, laborious, and fraught with the thorns and thistles of discomfort and uncertainty.

The pastoral staff of RAC have often reflected on the reality that in a truly multicultural church, because of the multiple diversities, about 20 percent of the people are uncomfortable roughly 80 percent of the time. As leadership in the community makes continual adjustments, the initial 20 percent may grow more comfortable, but then a new group becomes uncomfortable. This give-and-take is not always a process of elimination—a "musical chairs of discomfort," so to speak—but sharing the burden of discomfort, whether on occasion or quite often, is an essential commitment for those pursuing reconciliation in the real world.

In this way, becoming the beloved community is both a gift and a burden. It's a gift because this strange way of being family is of course in alignment with all the surprising reversal and creativity we find in God's kingdom. The blessing of the kingdom is revealed in the mysterious work of the Holy Spirit, who acts as a mediator to reconcile people who were formerly estranged. When we receive the loving gifts of the Spirit, our notions of "us" and "them" begin to look so small (even though our differences remain important in how we understand identity and community). Yet these gifts—much like God's grace, which we freely receive—are not cheap. They are indeed, as Dietrich Bonhoeffer reminds us, freely given and quite costly at the same time. This new family is hardly without its challenges and discouragements, and these costs can feel burdensome at times. But this burden is not an oppressive load; rather, it is the weight and responsibility of costly discipleship.

Ultimately, at Rainier Avenue Church, it seems to me that most of the habits of cultivation that have born the fruit of beloved community have come from understanding and inhabiting the local soil and not necessarily because people have a deep and holistic theology of reconciliation. What I mean is that the faithful practices of hospitality and fictive kinship have grown out of a natural awareness of, and attention to, the local, built environment. Around here, a lived theology of place that welcomes diverse neighbors generously is "in the water," and in some cases on the street corners whose names are etched on our buildings.

Rainier Avenue Refuge

A few years ago, I was attending our midweek Community Night program at RAC, and as usual, the mixed crowd was seated around large, round tables in the fellowship hall. Hot bowls of soup and many lively discussions filled the air with the aromas and sounds of warmth and activity. A visitor I didn't recognize was at my table, and so we quickly struck up a conversation about where he was from. The first thing I noticed about Marlo was his huge smile and infectious energy as he introduced himself with an enthusiastic handshake.

I asked Marlo how he first heard about RAC, and much to my surprise, he said he was actually just walking by one day and sort of stumbled in. More specifically, he went on to explain that he had recently been released from prison (he casually named the specific correctional facility), where he had become a devout Muslim and a leader in the prison's Islamic community, only to later turn to Christianity and renounce his Muslim faith. Talk about a transparent and interesting introduction!

The way he described it, Marlo was walking down Rainier Avenue one day and randomly encountered some former Muslim brothers who recognized him from prison. They confronted him about his conversion to Christianity, and unfortunately the situation began to escalate. Seeing that he was outnumbered, Marlo weighed his options and decided it would be best to avoid getting into a street fight. Looking around for a way to escape, he saw the Rainier Avenue Church building and ran through the open front door. He was basically looking for a safe place to wait things out and then be on his way.

"But I guess God had other plans," Marlo said. He quickly met a few people at the church and made some small talk, perhaps just killing time until the coast was clear. But the conversations must have struck a chord, and like so many before him, Marlo was greeted and welcomed warmly. After visiting on a following Sunday and taking a good look around, Marlo said to himself, "This seems like a place for me." Naturally, a big part of this welcome involved several church members lovingly coming alongside Marlo as he made some difficult adjustments to getting different pieces of his life back together. When his transitional housing situation fell through, one particular family even took Marlo in to live with them for over a year—a clear picture of genuine Christian hospitality!

As I learned more about Marlo's story and his passionate Christian faith, I was struck not only by his resilience and optimism, given the many hardships he'd faced in life (losing a son to gang violence, struggles with addiction), but also by his thoughtful and informed compassion for the many Muslims he met while incarcerated. Being a young black man in prison was obviously traumatic on its own, and dramatically parting ways with the Muslim community there had been really tough. But Marlo expressed a deep respect and appreciation for the earnest and rigorous discipline of the Muslim faith, even as he returned to the Christianity of his youth. Marlo saw his own journey as an opportunity to be a peacemaker and reconciler between Muslim and Christian communities.

Some more skeptical may have written off Marlo's upbeat enthusiasm as an act, but his joyful worship on Sunday mornings only seemed more genuine each week. He took the six-week membership class, served as a ministry volunteer, and generally just brightened the room. Unfortunately, as much as I wish I could say otherwise, there is no happy ending to this particular story. Despite some real progress in finding work and reconnecting with family, some of Marlo's darker struggles caught up with him in the end, and he tragically passed away in an unexpected incident. I deeply regret not being able to arrange his visit to my crosscultural ministry class like we had discussed, but I'll always remember Marlo's moving testimony, which he first shared with me at RAC's Community Night, and how our location on Rainier Avenue provided a place of refuge and worship for him, even if only for a short season.

I don't think Marlo's story would have been possible in most of the churches I know in Seattle, but it makes a lot of sense for those who understand RAC's history, identity, and values. Once again, the ways Marlo became a part of the RAC family, however briefly and imperfectly, were not the result of theoretical formulations of compassion or reconciliation. People did not take a class or read a textbook on welcoming the stranger where they would be convinced of a theological argument. Rather, the RAC family cared for Marlo and journeyed with him in hardship because they were committed to a place and to the many different people who share that place for better or worse.

When Marlo walked through the front doors of the church seeking refuge, he stepped into a long history of faithful presence in a uniquely diverse neighborhood. Like most other places, color lines and class divisions are always at work in our urban context, but those of us who call RAC home are trying to carve out some space on our street corner where the Spirit can mend and heal all that's been broken. Paying attention to our urban location is not just a part of the DNA at RAC; it's also the first step in embodying and reenacting the Christian story of incarnational humility and radical love of neighbor. The family that is formed in the process is sometimes a little strange or awkward, but if there's a picture of beloved community that I can actually imagine in real life, it looks a lot like Rainier Avenue Church.

Perhaps your church or faith community is not located on a street like Rainier Avenue, or maybe you have not yet taken more intentional steps to pay attention to your place in the neighborhood. There are still a lot of simple ways to begin the process, and most of them begin with assessing the opportunities for bridge building that are located nearby. What assets and deficits in your local community might create a natural context for dialogue and friendship with people who are different? As always, sometimes the most natural opportunities are right in front of us, or waiting next door.

When the leadership of Seattle Chinese Alliance Church (SCAC) began to ask some of these questions, they knew there was a diverse, underresourced elementary school right across the street. Over the course of a couple of years, and after many pizza parties, tutoring sessions, clothing drives, and summer programs, I think it's safe to say that the staff of Dearborn Park Elementary and the staff of SCAC have become friends. Last year, when Dearborn Park was low on funds and had to decide between staffing a counselor and buying printer paper, they chose the counselor because of the many family needs in the school. But in the same way many of us trust we can rely on our extended family, the school staff also knew they could reach out to their friends across the street—not only to meet an immediate need for supplies, but also to provide the relational support and encouragement every child needs to succeed.

The Welcoming Table

No description of the gospel story and its embodied life would be complete without one final family tradition: the table. The new community that is being formed in the life of the church is centered on the table in both common and profoundly significant ways. In social settings, the table is a shared, casual point of access for food, fellowship, and connecting with others over the most basic but essential human activities: eating, talking, and laughing. As a Chinese American, the importance of eating together goes far beyond the necessity of sustenance and the convenience of consuming food in the presence of others. A common Chinese greeting literally means "Have you eaten?" and there are many elaborate, though sometimes cumbersome, socially scripted rituals around offering, receiving, and enjoying different kinds of foods on different occasions. Regardless of the setting, I can appreciate the centrality of the table as a place for family intimacy and a metaphor for the importance of communal life.

But in the Christian story, there is also a deeper kind of hospitality happening at the sacred Table. The metaphor of the shared meal evokes all the rich memories of the tables set in Israel's story, from the deliverance in Egypt celebrated in the Passover meal to the intimate retelling of that story in the upper room on the night Jesus was betrayed. The Eucharist, the Lord's Supper, Holy Communion—or however you refer to the Table in your tradition—are all symbols of the same reconciling reality. Every person, however righteous or rejected, comes to the Table as a broken sinner in need of God's mercy and grace, made beautifully accessible in the common elements of bread and wine.

As Jesus takes these ordinary elements of bread—blessed, broken, and given—and wine poured out for others, a familiar story is being retold: all are invited to receive the gifts of God for the people of God. The offering is God's self for the brokenness of the world; Jesus' blood is shed for the forgiveness of many, regardless of their tribe, tongue, criminal history, or racial background. Again and again, as Jesus followers participate in the ritual of this Table, they are formed into a family of invitation and belonging, a Table where the wrong kinds of people have always gathered to celebrate and receive the feast of God's grace. Apparently, in this strange family, traitors, tax collectors, hustlers, dealers, common folk, deacons, and elders all belong to one another. Both the religiously destitute and those impoverished in spirit are welcome. Difficult as it may be to believe and even harder to put into practice, these people belong around the same Table, dining, discerning, and communing.

In this way, the local church needs to practice both the common table of hospitality and the sacred Table of God's reconciling grace, because these two dimensions of the table are interdependent. Welcoming neighbors to the table of fellowship makes space for friendship in times of celebration and solidarity in times of struggle. The more the church cultivates this hospitable space—locally, regularly, and faithfully—the more the neighborhood recognizes the Christian community as a place of genuine care and mutual support. Subsequently, as this place of welcome grows in relationship and trust, a worshiping life centered on the sacred Table allows this foundational practice to frame why we gather. In turn, by partaking in the life-giving elements of the Table, the community is empowered to offer this grace to a wider circle of neighbors and with a deeper commitment to love, belonging, and justice. This is the sacramental life of the church in the city.

The local church needs to practice both the common table of hospitality and the sacred Table of God's reconciling grace, because these two dimensions of the table are interdependent.

Charles Marsh describes this beloved community as

> the new social space inaugurated by the great event of the cross where all people are invited to partake in the welcoming table of God. Here we share common cause in a common struggle. Here we borrow each hope from our brothers and sisters and children for a better future. Here we work for mercy and justice in what Dr. King called "the fierce urgency of now." Here we learn to dwell in the radiant peace of Christ.[5]

In this sense, the Table is a comfort that welcomes and also a discomfort that all are not yet welcome. As we enjoy the fellowship of extended family, we must also be animated and energized to enlarge the table and increase its reach in communities divided by patterns of exclusion. Making space for those who have not yet come to feast on God's goodness is at times a delicate balancing act between invitation and agitation.

Reverend John Helmiere, who I mentioned briefly at the end of the last chapter, is the convener and minister of listening at Valley and Mountain Fellowship, one of the communities that anchors their change-making space, the Collaboratory. In addition to hosting regular meals throughout the week that are free and open to all, John knows the welcoming table is not only for holding potlucks and barbecues. Valley and Mountain folks also participate in regular "Table Turning Mondays," where together they gather in the spirit of Jesus' temple cleansing to stand against greedy profiteering and unjust systems such as mass incarceration that exploit the poor. Activism without fellowship is what Dr. Cornel West sometimes calls "motion without movement,"[6] but turning over unjust tables because we've been welcomed to the most generous Table of all is the natural outcome of the ethics of Christian friendship.

As we look ahead, let us not confuse the radical hospitality of the Table for a sentimental moment of inclusivity, the kind we see so carefully manicured in diverse marketing materials and feel-good entertainment. Christians must remember that the story of reconciliation we are striving to inhabit is truly beautiful and entirely disruptive at the same time. After all, what could be more beautifully disruptive than a peculiar community where God is sowing seeds of love and belonging into the soils of discord and division?

- 8 -

Getting Practical

Action and Reflection

I sometimes struggle to do two things at once. Beyond walking and chewing gum, my multitasking skills are limited, even though I occasionally try to convince myself that I'm being more productive. Usually, it's better if I focus on one thing at a time before I move on to something else. But what if tasks that seem more singular are actually layered processes with deeper mechanics at work below the surface?

Consider the relatively simple (or so it may seem) task of hitting a baseball. On one level, mechanically, there's not a whole going on—the goal is to accurately position the bat to make solid contact with the ball in order to send it in a desired direction. Mastering this skill does take significant effort and practice, but the task itself, which occurs in an instant, may seem like a singular act of athletic coordination, or what some call muscle memory.

However, studying great hitters at the highest levels of the game reveals a deeper process at work that's hidden in the fraction of a second it takes to hit a homerun. Professional baseball players are aware of a myriad of factors in the moments before a swing: their breathing, body position, grip on the bat, the subtleties of a pitcher's wind-up, the sound of the ball cutting through the air, and so forth. Top athletes aiming to optimize their skills are not simply honing an innate reflex; often they are practicing an intentional awareness and *mindfulness* that provides the foundation for peak performance. In short, these athletes are practicing the integration of action and reflection.

Impractical Theology?

In the academic world, I've always been amused by the fact that my field of expertise (intercultural studies and missiology) often falls into a larger category of *practical* theology, mostly just to distinguish the kind of work I do from that of biblical scholars, historians, or systematic theologians. While I'm not a big fan of the silo effect these categories create, I do understand and generally support the organizing principles. With that said, before we get practical, as this chapter's title suggests, I want to press—however briefly—the meaning of theological practicality for a moment.

The theory-practice divide is an old debate I won't rehash here, even though its concerns—the ever-present and growing gap between academics and the church—remain as relevant and urgent as ever. But we need to recognize the importance of holding action and reflection *together*. The impulse and resolve to *act*—to show up, speak out, and get involved—is absolutely essential to the Christian faith. What is theology if not a *lived* faith in word and deed? Many young people I teach and serve are often challenging me (and rightfully so) to get out there, engage, and "walk the talk." Too many academics are comfortable in world of ideas without having to put them into practice, and that's problematic on a number of levels.

However, though this critique of theological inaction can be valid, I also want to emphasize the importance of deep, critical reflection in the life of faith, of paying closer attention to our actions as we bring an intentional and spiritual mindfulness to whatever our practical work entails. Action for activity's sake can be aimless or counterproductive, and as was previously mentioned, social *motion* and social *movement* are not the same thing. Some activists may be inadvertently generating a lot of motion and commotion without necessarily laying the groundwork that sustains a true movement.

Thus, a synthesis of active reflection *and* reflective action is always the most practical thing to do. By practical we mean the practices that produce lasting and meaningful change in both the life of the individual practitioner *and* the community in which they serve. Practical application of theology should never operate like the easy how-to lists that come with numbered directions in an instruction manual. Discipleship simply does not work that way, and when reduced to such mechanics, the real power and efficacy of Christian formation in society is lost.

Brazilian educator Paulo Freire called this synthesis of action and reflection *praxis*. By holding active reflection and reflective action together in critical dialogue, social realities and contexts (i.e., people, places, and societies) could be transformed and liberated from the bottom up and from the inside out.[1] Christian praxis holds a similar view: when thoughtful and committed Christians resolve to practice an informed and reflective faith, their embodied actions point to the kind of transforming and liberating power of the gospel as expressed by Jesus in Luke 4:18-19:

The Spirit of the Lord is on me,
  because he has anointed me
  to proclaim good news to the poor.
He has sent me to proclaim freedom for the prisoners
  and recovery of sight for the blind,
to set the oppressed free,
  to proclaim the year of the Lord's favor.

Ironically, despite the weight and significance of this well-known gospel proclamation, many scholars agree that the year of the Lord's favor—the Jubilee year—and its radical social and economic restructuring of society was never fully realized in Israel. Why was canceling debt, returning capital resources, and essentially leveling the economic playing field so difficult? Explanations vary, but they mostly seem to suggest that the practices of Jubilee were simply too theoretical, idealistic, and far-reaching. Treating workers fairly, lending without interest, welcoming foreigners, and the redistribution of land, labor, and resources was just too impractical. How could people be convinced that these radical ethics were a good, attainable idea?

It's not hard to imagine the reluctance of people in Israel in the face of Jubilee's costly demands. Rationalizations for supporting the status quo and arguments for more moderate, realistic policies were surely suggested. Practicing socioeconomic reconciliation as a symbol of social holiness and an act of atonement for the sins of greed and its effects of maldistribution may have seemed like a nice idea *in theory*, but not so easy in practice. And yet, from the perspective of Christian praxis, what could be more right than the year of Jubilee and its reversal of the injustices of accumulation and excess? What could be a better synthesis of action and reflection than a collective commitment to liberation for the poor and oppressed as an act of righteousness and worship?

The complex work set before us in reconciling race and place absolutely requires practical engagement, but we cannot substitute easy solutions for the hard work of genuinely reflective action. The challenging processes of place making, hospitality, and community building in the midst of structural exclusion are daunting to say the least, but reflecting on the nature of faithful Christian praxis may just be the right place to begin.

The Social Logic of Homogeneity

We've covered a lot of ground on this journey to reconciliation. Early on we used the phrase "social logic of homogeneity." This cultural tendency is not as complex as it sounds. The social logic is simply a rationale of comfort and safety in settings with people that are familiar. It's a desire for homogeneity or uniformity that shapes the location and social composition of our circles of friends and those we trust. We cluster into groups of similarity for all kinds of reasons: to form and affirm our identity, make communication and share culture more easily, and provide a kind of social and psychological safety net when we encounter conflict that we don't understand. This logic is why we live where we live, shop where we shop, worship where we worship, and even love who we love.

But we've also seen the underside of homogeneity on a structural and systemic level. The blatantly racialized history of land, housing, and education—and subsequently, suburbs, wealth, and opportunity, and now gentrification. These patterns of homogeneity, masked with platitudes like "separate but equal," created exclusive privileges for many (a mortgage, home equity, and upward mobility) and dead-end cycles for others (public housing, generational poverty, and institutional dependence). After decades of an uneven playing field and the ongoing entrenchment of racially biased policies, is it any wonder that today's suggestions of colorblindness reek of hypocrisy and ignorance?

Law professor John A. Powell puts it this way:

> At one point, we had explicit laws that said "whites are on top and blacks are on the bottom." Today we have many of the same practices without the explicit language. And those practices are largely inscribed in geography. So geography does the work of Jim Crow laws. Many people are

> confused—why after 50 years of Civil Rights are our schools, housing markets, and jobs still segregated? A lot of this is a function of how we've re-inscribed the racial-geographic space in the United States. That structure is still what we're living in today.[2]

Simply put, social homogeneity on a small scale is understandable and even necessary for society. But left to its own devices, when allowed to run rampant without questioning its costs, the social logic of homogeneity snowballs to become a policy-laden behemoth that runs roughshod over others, often under the guise of stability, security, or efficiency. Large populations of sameness, now with the power of resources, fall into the predictable fallacies of groupthink, ethnocentrism, xenophobia, and cultural appropriation.

After the unarmed, teenage Michael Brown was fatally shot in the streets of Ferguson, Missouri, by a white police officer, many people on opposite sides of the color line came to—unsurprisingly—totally opposite conclusions about what had occurred. In the wake of the shooting, racial tensions flared that are still inflamed today, and research about divergent perspectives was telling. Robert Jones of the Public Religion Research Institute describes how

When allowed to run rampant without questioning its costs, the social logic of homogeneity snowballs to become a policy-laden behemoth that runs roughshod over others, often under the guise of stability, security, or efficiency.

> the chief obstacle to having an intelligent, or even intelligible, conversation across the racial divide is that white Americans live in communities that face far fewer problems and talk mostly to other white people. . . . Overall, the social networks of whites are a remarkable 91

> percent white. In fact, fully 75 percent of whites have entirely white social networks without any minority presence. This level of social-network racial homogeneity among whites is significantly higher than among black Americans or Hispanic Americans.[3]

Sadly, here the basic but deeply flawed outcome of the social logic of homogeneity is on full display: when people remain socially, geographically, and personally segregated from racial difference, the chasm of racial misunderstanding and conflict naturally widens.

Social psychologist Christena Cleveland identifies these divisive phenomena as "the sinister effects of normal categorizing—inaccurate perceptions . . . false interpretations and memories, group polarization, and perspective divergence," and then goes on to explain how they "are working to maintain homogeneous groups and widen the divide."[4] While the logical and most effective solution to these divisions is prolonged, meaningful, and relational experiences with others (with the specific intention of understanding their experiences and perspectives), this is unfortunately much easier said than done. Once again, we bump up against the obstacles of geography. Like all US cities, the St. Louis metro area in general and Ferguson in particular both have long histories of racially restrictive housing covenants, redlining in real estate, residential segregation in housing and wealth, and racially homogeneous, low-performing public schools.

In fact, ProPublica researchers remind us that "the Normandy school district from which Michael Brown graduated is among the poorest and most segregated in Missouri. It ranks last in overall academic performance. Its rating on an annual state assessment was so dismal that by the time Brown graduated the district had lost its accreditation. About half of black male students at Normandy High never graduate."[5] Is it any surprise that young black men in Ferguson and around the nation are crowding the streets, screaming in desperation that their lives matter? But the utter failure of public education for literally millions of black and brown students in poor neighborhoods across the country barely registers on the public conscience of so many with privilege.

This is the cold, logical outcome of social homogeneity: out of sight, out of mind. If it doesn't affect me directly or at least become noticeable in contexts I recognize, then it's someone else's problem. Even better yet, I can absolve myself of any responsibility by using justifications that my homogeneous in-group has validated internally (e.g., victim blaming). Michael Brown simply should have studied harder, made better decisions, and been a more upstanding, responsible individual, right? When our perspectives originate from the same vantage point, then it's easy to agree. And when we're all in agreement with each other, then we naturally see things the same way. This circular logic breeds insularity, confirmation bias (interpretations that confirm our preconceived notions), and social isolation.

By now, I hope the patterns are plainly obvious. Racial segregation in Ferguson, Detroit, Chicago, Los Angeles, New York, Memphis, Milwaukee, Baltimore, and Seattle parallels the kinds of ethnic and cultural tensions we see in Paris, Beijing, Sao Paulo, and Nairobi. The cycles of social homogeneity spiral into predictable patterns all over the world's urban landscapes. Ghettos and gated communities, barrios and bank towers, slums and five-star resorts coexist and perpetuate one another, but remain carefully segregated from each other by physical walls, class boundaries, and racial barriers. What can we do to *unlearn* the social logic of homogeneity that has wreaked so much havoc in our neighborhoods and cities? How can communities of diverse belonging take root on the fault lines where divisions fragment society? These are the two central questions as we move toward a Christian praxis of reflecting and acting on race and place.

Undoing and Relearning

When I first learned to play the guitar as a teenage hobby one summer, I was quite proud of myself for figuring it out on my own with the help of a few chord sheets and diagrams. As I got better and my interest grew, I decided to try out for my high school's jazz band, which meant I would need to take some lessons to learn the scales and music theory that are foundational to jazz. But since I already knew how to play (or so I thought), I figured it shouldn't be too difficult. What's so hard about a few new chords and some jazzy accents?

Those of you familiar with jazz may already realize how wrong I was. When I met my teacher for the first lesson, I confidently assured him that I was self-taught and wouldn't need to start at the beginning. He smiled knowingly, and then proceeded to spend nearly the entire first lesson on tuning. Yes, we spent about forty-five minutes getting the six strings of our Stratocasters in sync, and that was pretty much it for the day. It probably would have taken less time if not for the fact that my ear had not been trained to hear the waves and tone of every note to the precise tolerances I would need to master in order to learn jazz.

Subsequent weeks felt painfully slow, mostly because I had to *unlearn* all the "skills" I had supposedly taught myself. My finger positions were off, I held my pick the wrong way, and my sense of syncopated rhythms—while functional—needed a lot of work. My patient teacher worked with me to gradually correct all my bad habits and tendencies because the higher-level skills I would really need to succeed at jazz would depend on a solid foundation of the basic skills. In essence, I had to totally undo the ways I had practiced for so long in order to relearn the right way to play the guitar.

Similarly, if we are going to make a serious attempt at practicing Christian reconciliation the right way, then we'll need to go back to the beginning and get our fundamentals right. The comforts of sameness and uniformity have caused us to pick up some bad habits, and unlearning the social logic of homogeneity in order to move toward communities of belonging will take some real time and effort. We can't simply add some nice activities on top of a host of deeply ingrained practices that got us started on the wrong foot to begin with.

Like brushing over a peeling paint job or building on top of a crooked foundation, the bad stuff underneath will always resurface eventually, or worse, lead to the whole thing toppling over. As we've repeatedly emphasized, if our roots aren't healthy, then our fruits won't be, either. We have to relearn how to cultivate communities from the seedbed; we can't sow homogeneous exclusion and then expect to reap diverse belonging. First we need to weed the garden, and then we can replant.

So the following postures and practices of place are in one sense nothing innovative or paradigm shifting on the surface; they may seem more like basic skills than complex solutions. But the longer I spend in active reflection about the interrelated problems of racialization, structural exclusion, and the comfortable patterns of uniformity, the more I'm convinced that we need a deep, foundational reboot of sorts. We've got to unlearn in order to relearn, and doing so takes us back to the not-so-simple questions we asked in the beginning:

If we are going to make a serious attempt at practicing Christian reconciliation the right way, then we'll need to go back to the beginning and get our fundamentals right.

- Where do you experience belonging and why?

- With whom do you identify, and what does that mean for racial others?
- How have you located your life—residentially, socially, and vocationally—in ways that may simply reinforce your preconceived understandings of identity and community?

My hope is that these "back-to-basics" questions will help us get to the heart of the matter: that moving from estrangement and exclusion to family and belonging will require the intentionality of presence, a commitment to rereading and relocating, and the creativity of social imagination.

Showing Up: The Ministry of Presence

It's perhaps been overstated that consistently showing up is a big part of success, but by showing up, I do not mean simply occupying space in a particular location. For most of us, it's relatively easy to passively suck air somewhere, but that usually isn't the beginning of anything especially significant. However, there's a big difference between showing up with minimal effort or attention and showing up while being fully and intentionally *present*. Every week I work with classrooms full of college students, some of whom are fully present in mind, body, and soul, while others seem to give just the minimal amount of attention to maintain consciousness and avoid being called on to answer a question.

One of the things I'll always remember about my friend Chad Anderson is that he lived a life of intentional presence, and whenever he showed up somewhere—for a neighborhood gathering, a prayer meeting, or a one-on-one conversation—he was truly and fully there. Chad was attentive, engaged, and invested in the moment at hand. Sometimes talking with Chad required your full attention as well because his voice was so soft, mostly due to some physical limitations from a rare brain tumor that Chad had defiantly overcome since childhood. The tumor may have restricted his balance and mobility, but it never limited his willingness to be present with people. Chad effortlessly demonstrated the interpersonal gift of hospitality; people always felt seen, heard, and truly listened to in Chad's welcoming presence.

When Chad and his wife, Melinda, moved to southeast Seattle as a part of our intentional southside community group, they dove headfirst into the local neighborhood, quickly putting down roots and joining with others in community clean-ups, the shared work of neighborhood associations, and of course the occasional march or gathering at city hall. Even when this involved uncomfortable moments, such as finding a handgun at the bus stop, or being on the receiving end of a drive-by yelling of "gentrification!" Chad seemed to take it all in stride. Being a young white guy in a historically black neighborhood wasn't always easy, but Chad always listened carefully and thoughtfully. Despite the fact that his mobility was limited by bus routes and scooter accessibility, Chad always found a way to get around, get involved, and show up wherever he needed to be a good neighbor.

Meanwhile, the things Chad and Melinda were learning in the hood were also translating into their family life. Chad grew up on the mission field as a third-culture kid in various West African locations, so when he and Melinda prayerfully decided to commit to becoming foster parents and they were presented with the opportunity to welcome two Congolese teenagers, they faithfully jumped again into another adventure of becoming a new kind of family. The beauty, hospitality, and humor of the Anderson household was not lost on their friends and neighbors.

After Chad tragically passed away in an unexpected medical incident, hundreds of friends, family, and neighbors from near and far gathered for his memorial service to grieve his loss and celebrate his life. The service was remarkable for many reasons, but I was especially struck by the many neighbors who came to share what Chad meant to them. These were not just family members or friends from the church communities where Chad had worshiped; these were the people who lived next door to Chad and Melinda, or the other neighbors who often ran into Chad on the sidewalk, at the bus stop, or in community meetings.

Person after person shared how Chad noticed them, welcomed them, listened to them, shared with them, and loved them. In what is sure to become a part of Chad's enduring legacy, even the mailman cried when he learned that Chad was gone. The mailman! Hearing all of this was both inspiring and challenging. I was inspired because here was Chad, who faced a lifetime of physical challenges that would have certainly defeated me and my concern for others. But these so-called limitations seemingly emboldened Chad to love more freely, smile more often, and simply be the kind of neighbor whose absence is now sorely felt by so many. Chad was far from perfect, but in all the ways and places he had located his life, he faithfully showed up again and again—as a husband, father, son, brother, mentor, neighbor, and friend—and his humble, loving presence left an indelible mark on the lives of those who knew him.

Chad's remarkable life also leaves us with some challenging questions. My wife, Chris, and I have been reflecting on our own family's neighborly witness—what would people say about us if we were gone? Would *our* next-door neighbors come to speak out about how present, thoughtful, compassionate, and welcoming we were? Would people from near and far—from all different racial, cultural, and religious backgrounds—come to share about how our family showed up, made space at our table, and sought the peace of the city (Jer 29:7)?

The physical limitations that Chad faced also gave him the gift of paying attention to those on the margins. Chad knew all too well what it felt like to be different, unheard, or ignored, and so throughout his life, he went looking for opportunities to connect with people on the outside, those on the fringes of the places where we normally fix our attention. Too many of us have been socially and culturally conditioned to focus on the center, where the bright lights and desirable life experiences allegedly occur. As we've seen, we're subconsciously captive to these instinctual tendencies and habits, mostly because the powerful societal streams around us envelop our lives in a current of accumulation and homogeneity. The places where we imagine the good life are so often just fabricated reconstructions of our own self-affirming desires.

But I genuinely believe that Chad—like others who have been "afflicted"—saw the life of faith from a different location. And so the persistence and perseverance of showing up that characterized his life came from a different picture of the good life and took Chad into the geographies of grace we discover in God's kingdom. It's there that we unlearn our fears of danger and difference and relearn the real meaning of community and obedience. How will we take up the challenge to listen more intentionally, to practice the ministry of presence, and to live in the places where our neighbors are longing to be seen and heard? If there's anything I learned from Chad, I think it starts with showing up.

Rereading at the Margins

In addition to the ministry of presence, which is more of a posture than a practice, a second perspective on practices of place involves a relocation of sorts, or at the very least, a rereading of our social location from a new and different position.

Rereading at the margins is a practice of shifting horizons; it is an intentional move toward the marginal space that most often remains on the periphery of our vision. These forgotten and ignored places—communities of incarceration, deportation, transience, and addiction—are kept invisible to soothe our public conscience and maintain perceived moral boundaries between so-called mainstream and marginal people.

As long as the boundaries remain in place, we can uphold the logic of social homogeneity and believe that we belong at the center with those who are like us—morally, politically, and racially. In contexts of homogeneity, the center is always the dominant culture, and the geography of the majority is shaped by those dominant, controlling interests. Thus, an intentional repositioning to the marginal space on the outside is an attempt at seeing and reading the center from the periphery, or *rereading* spaces of dominance from places of exclusion and suffering. What does a prison look like from the inside, and how do the incarcerated view the people and systems on the outside?

Rereading at the margins is a practice of shifting horizons; it is an intentional move toward the marginal space that most often remains on the periphery of our vision.

In the first chapter, we explored the idea of *cultural exegesis*, or reading and interpreting cultural texts in cities for the "signs of the times." Whenever we read closely and critically, French philosopher Paul Ricoeur reminds us that one of the things we have to keep in mind is not only the world *of* the text (and *behind* the text) but also the world *in front of* the text—that is, the world of the reader, whose interpretive lens is always shaped by a particular location and context.[6] When I read a map, it certainly helps to know my own location so I can get to wherever I'm going. But without knowing where I am, it's hard to make sense of the map's meaning.

In the same way, when I read the Christian Scriptures, I bring my social location to the meaning of the text. As an English-speaking Asian American, an educated reader, and a straight, married male in my late thirties, I bring various lenses to the text as I interpret what it says. But what happens when my location shifts? How will the meaning shift accordingly? One of my favorite books on this topic is Bob Ekblad's *Reading the Bible with the Damned*, which describes a journey of "descent into the suffering world," from the poor *campesinos* of Honduras to immigrants and inmates in the Skagit County Jail, about sixty miles north of Seattle.[7]

After years of teaching sustainable farming and facilitating grassroots Bible studies with Honduran peasants, Bob and Gracie Ekblad moved to the Skagit Valley, an agricultural region that draws many migrant laborers from Mexico and Central America for farm work. The ecumenical ministry they founded is called Tierra Nueva (New Earth) and works primarily with people on the margins, such as undocumented immigrants or those caught up in the criminal justice system. When their ministry began in the Skagit Valley in 1994, one of the first places Bob served was as the chaplain at the Skagit County Jail, where today he continues to walk with people who are suffering from addiction, racial and economic injustice, and the vicious cycles of gang violence.

The life and character of the vibrant Tierra Nueva community has been shaped around its values of God's freedom for the oppressed and a concern for the places where people on the margins are suffering. It is difficult to imagine their ministry apart from the particular landscapes and locations of its people, from jail cells and courtrooms to the potato fields and living rooms of migrant farm workers and their families. As Bob has described his own journey, throughout his life, he found that his own sense of alienation within mainstream Christianity helped him to identify with outsiders and led him into places and communities of marginalization and exclusion wherever he was. Underneath it all was a desire to realize the good news of God's healing and liberation for saints and sinners alike.

In essence, Bob saw that where his life was located needed a social and geographic adjustment in order for him to make sense of the good news of the kingdom that Jesus preached. So he followed the geography of God's gracious concern for the poor to Honduras, to France, and then back to the Pacific Northwest, but in every place he returned to the same questions: How can people on the margins experience the goodness and freedom of God? And how can mainstream Christians come alongside those who are suffering in order to become a beloved community where *mutual* liberation and salvation can be experienced by both the privileged and the powerless?

How can mainstream Christians come alongside those who are suffering in order to become a beloved community where *mutual* liberation and salvation can be experienced by both the privileged and the powerless?

A couple of years ago, I visited Bob at Tierra Nueva, and he was showing me the Underground Coffee Project, a unique partnership between Honduran coffee growers and Tierra Nueva's gang and exoffender ministry, where exoffenders are becoming artisan coffee roasters and social entrepreneurs. As we moved down into the basement of the building, just below the space where the worshiping community meets every Sunday for the Word and Table, I could smell the rich aroma of freshly roasting coffee beans wafting up the stairs. The coffee-roasting space was small but organized, and as the beans were being roasted and turned, two workers were off to the side on a weight bench. They smiled and greeted us but didn't get up from the bench because they were in the process of tattooing. As Bob inquired with a friendly curiosity, they explained their latest ink.

The guy giving the tattoo was a former Mexican gang member recently released from years in prison. He had come to faith through Tierra Nueva's jail and prison ministry and has become an outreach worker with Tierra Nueva's gang and exoffender ministry. The guy receiving the tattoo then casually described—in between wincing at the needle—that he was a former neo-Nazi skinhead, and as such he had a lot of tattoos of swastikas and other white supremacist imagery, which he was trying to get rid of since becoming a Christian at Tierra Nueva. But some of the older ink was hard to remove, so he was getting new work to cover up the old—a rose in place of racist tattoos from his past. The whole conversation was rather nonchalant, as if this kind of occurrence was just another ordinary day at Tierra Nueva.

It's hard for me to imagine a more beautiful picture of the gospel than a flower blooming over the scars of hatred and exclusion because of the new life of the Spirit at work underneath the church. Is there any clearer image of what Paul declares about the ministry of reconciliation in 2 Corinthians 5:17? "If anyone is in Christ, the new creation has come: The old has gone, the new is here!" This story of underground transformation is exactly the place where communities of belonging are being formed across the deep divisions of race and class. In the marginal space of the Skagit Valley, where exoffenders and undocumented laborers meet together for fellowship, those who have been excluded by the racial prejudices of criminality and illegality can gather at the Table to experience the freedom of God's gracious welcome.

Mainstream Christians at the center of the dominant culture, where social homogeneity reigns, need to unlearn and undo their isolation from suffering and excluded communities through rereading at the margins. Only by repositioning their geographic horizons will churches begin to genuinely move toward a sense of belonging that does not dismiss or exclude racial others because of moral or legal qualifiers that only hold sway "from a worldly point of view" (2 Cor 5:16). It will not be easy to unlearn the old habits of fear and condemnation that hold us captive to our more judgmental impulses, but I'm confident that the beginning of identifying with those on the margins requires a step of faith in the right direction that moves us toward a new horizon of possibility in God's kingdom. Just as Bob discovered so many years ago through reading the Bible with the incarcerated, things simply look different when we place our lives on the dividing lines of society and then venture across into new territory to make a home and a family with those we find on the other side.

Acting and Reflecting for Change

At this point in the conversation about a Christian praxis of race and place, it may still feel like the practicality of active reflection and reflective action is a bit difficult to get our hands around, and that's understandable. The elusive nature of the way praxis works is in a dialogical tension, which means we're in a constant state of acting and reflecting at the same time. This may sound exhausting, and at times it can be, but it is also liberating because we are freed from the unrealistic expectations of following some instructions and then expecting neat and clean resolutions.

Like anything that's worth striving and struggling for, the changes we are seeking in contexts of division are as much about ourselves as they are about society at large. The patterns of exclusion we've examined in cities and beyond are simply magnifications of our deep-seated fears and insecurities about each other and about life together. If we're going to pursue a different way forward in the direction of communities of belonging, then our place making and family forming will require both personal, spiritual transformation and structural, societal change. Reconciliation has always worked this way. in the small, incremental changes of our character and inward life as well as the large, aggregated effects of communities like the local church who come together with and for their neighbors.

Thankfully, the Holy Spirit is at work in both realms, inviting us into contemplation and animating us for activism. It is truly a gift we must step back and receive that Jesus, the Great Reconciler, is not limited by fatigue, confusion, despair, or institutional obstacles.

Conclusion

Back to a New Beginning

In the first chapter, I described my journey down the cold, neglected streets of Detroit in the winter of 2010. As the funeral procession drove through the infamous color line of 8 Mile Road, my grandfather's death felt heavier still with the sadness of urban decay. But in contrast to those darker memories, I can also remember that my grandfather's life was full of vitality and creativity. He was born in a poor, coastal village in Toishan, southern China, in 1915 and immigrated to Detroit in 1939. As a young man with a growing family in the city, he diligently ran a Chinese hand-laundry business (one of the few jobs open to Chinese immigrants then), raised three kids in the house behind the shop, and eventually retired to enjoy his hobbies of gardening, painting, and Chinese operas. Throughout my childhood, whenever we would visit, he was always working on a new project—an elaborate mural in the basement, a trellis for fruit in the garden, or a rousing rendition of his favorite operas recorded on VHS. We treasure these memories still.

In an interesting coincidence, renowned Chinese American activist and philosopher Grace Lee was also born in 1915, and her family also hailed from Toishan, where many of the earliest

Chinese immigrants to the United States trace their lineage to. Grace Lee controversially crossed multiple color lines in 1953 to marry Jimmy Boggs, an African American labor activist and auto worker, and they moved to Detroit to join in the civil rights movement. Like my grandfather, Grace Lee Boggs's life was also full of vitality and creativity, but unlike my grandfather, she never retired. The wide-reaching impact of her legacy in Detroit and beyond far outweighed her diminutive frame.

Another World Is Possible

Simply put, the courage and creativity of Grace Lee Boggs's social imagination was on another level of activism. When she completed her PhD in philosophy from Byrn Mawr College in 1940, Martin Luther King Jr. was still in elementary school. She organized with Malcolm X in the streets of Detroit in the 1960s and marched for civil rights, Black Power, and fair labor. When reflecting on Boggs's life, biographer Scott Kurashige asks, "Is there any other figure in the United States today who can reflect on seven decades of activist life and history with the vibrancy of Grace Lee Boggs? . . . She embodies the unity of theory and practice in a manner that has become increasingly rare."[1]

As a philosopher, feminist, and neighborly activist for the world, Grace was truly ahead of her time. Despite facing many professional obstacles, cultural and gender norms, and racial boundaries that easily could have derailed her passion, she pressed on and persevered through Detroit's darkest years, even when others had given up. She continually asserted that "Detroit is a city of Hope rather than a city of Despair. The thousands of vacant lots and abandoned houses provide not only the space to begin anew but also the incentive to create innovative ways of making our living—ways that nurture our most productive, cooperative, and caring selves."[2] In seeing what others couldn't, Grace imagined and realized innovative, place-based initiatives that were rooted in the arts, environmental care, and leadership development.

In 1992, shortly after the Los Angeles riots, Grace and Jimmy Boggs began a new project called Detroit Summer. It began in a church basement downtown "to engage young people in the movement to create this new kind of city . . . a multicultural, intergenerational youth program/movement to rebuild, redefine, and *respirit* Detroit from the ground up."[3] As a wise and seasoned social activist, Grace was not enamored with motion over movement, so Detroit Summer was intentionally narrow and deep in its approach. By working on a small scale, Grace said, "We could pay much closer and greater attention to the relationships we were building among ourselves and with communities in Detroit and beyond. The result has been that we have been able to develop the type of critical connections—of both ideas and people—that are the essential ingredients of building a movement."[4]

Ultimately, in addition to her clear commitment to action and reflection, Grace frequently turned to creativity and imagination as the catalysts for liberation from the destructive cycles of economic self-interest. She knew that communities like Detroit "need artists to create new images that will liberate us from our preoccupation with constantly expanding production and consumption, and open up space in our hearts and minds to imagine and create."[5] For Grace, neighborhood revitalization was never about flashy, high-profile investments whose profits tended to rise to the top. Instead, her imagination ran in the other direction, toward community gardens, neighborhood schools, and the richness of relationships cultivated through personal connections.

Grace never shied away from speaking her mind, even when her opinions were unpopular. In the midst of large-scale corporate proposals for urban revitalization, she saw another way forward:

> As I witness and participate in our visionary efforts to revitalize Detroit and contrast them with the multibillion dollars' worth of megaprojects advanced by politicians and developers that involve casinos, giant stadiums, gentrification, and the Super Bowl, I am saddened by their shortsightedness. At the same time I rejoice in the energy being unleashed in the community by our human-scale programs that involve bringing the country back into the city and removing the walls between schools and communities, between generations, and between ethnic groups. . . . Both for our livelihood and for our humanity we need to see progress not in terms of "having more" but in terms of growing our souls by creating community.[6]

The striking similarities between Grace Lee Boggs's activism and the various metaphors we've explored throughout the book remind me that creative partnerships are vital to the practices of place that cultivate a kingdom imagination. She may not have explicitly named the mustard seed, the upside-down kingdom, or the Christian disciplines of prayer and contemplation, but if there was ever an example of seeking the shalom of the city in a place of urban exile, it seems to me that Grace Lee Boggs's legacy has much to offer the church. As a Chinese American woman who committed her life to a place and a people who were not—by the world's standards—her own, Grace embodied a life of radical belonging.

Thanks to Grace and those like her, Detroit, like other "abandoned places of the empire,"[7] is not lost. Despite all appearances, disastrous racial exclusion and the legacies of structural injustice have not blotted out hope and creativity on the streets today where the Boggs Center continues its work just a few miles down the road from where my grandfather used to run his laundry. Admirers from near and far—students, politicians, and activists young and old—still visit the Boggs Center to recapture a vision for their own neighborhoods. Many sat with Grace around the table to laugh, learn, and dream; she was as active and imaginative as ever well into her late nineties. She served Detroit for sixty-two years and died at the young age of one hundred—a race well run.

The Gift of Christian Imagination

We began this journey with a few seminal words from Dr. Willie Jennings, who reminded us that "the story of race is also the story of place."[8] He challenged imaginative Christians "to transgress the boundaries of real estate, by buying where we should not and living where we must not, by living together where we supposedly cannot, and being identified with those whom we should not."[9] I hope our many excursions and wanderings through the various urban landscapes of cities, valleys, and street corners have demonstrated that these transgressions are indeed possible and even necessary.

Christian discipleship in our racial world is fraught with difficulties, and we've seen those challenges in so many different forms, from the basic impulses of social uniformity to the complex patterns and structures of historic policies that have evolved to exclude and exploit. As you witness these oppressive systems at work in your own neighborhood and reflect on these personal tendencies in your own life, I hope you'll never look at another freeway, public school, or suburban home the same way again. Beyond those new ways of seeing, I also pray that you'll be disturbed with our complicity in these problematic walls of hostility, to the point of further study, research, contemplation, and lament. May we hunger and thirst for righteousness and justice on our way to becoming children of God who inherit the kingdom.

But above all else, I hope that you'll discover the truly remarkable gift of Christian imagination that transforms people and places when we join with others in the joyful work of belonging to one another. Race is a social construction that continues to divide and conquer in our society, and we must take it seriously as a cultural, political, and theological problem. But we will not overcome the perils of racism with the tools of the world alone. As important as social awareness, grassroots education, passionate activism, and political power are, the nature of our task is cultivated in different soil and rooted in a different story.

The story to which we belong is dark at many points, but as the Word-made-flesh reminds us, "the darkness has not overcome it." In between the dark and low places are moments of grace and rays of hope, though they sometimes seem few and far between. But taken together, the gentle whisper of the Spirit and the generative power of diverse belonging become more than life rafts in an ocean of suffering; they are in fact the faithful beginnings of Christian community.

Christian community requires faithful imagination and creative perseverance to realize, but when we sit together in fellowship at the Table of hospitality, where all are truly welcome, we are overwhelmed with the reconciling love of God, which draws near to us and our neighbors. This doesn't happen in an instant, and the path of life together obviously gets rocky at times. Yet our world desperately needs those who are willing to travel this journey together.

Acknowledgments

As the title suggests, this book has been a journey in several dimensions. From proposal to publication, I'm truly grateful for the support and companionship of various travel partners. Many thanks to Helen Lee, Elissa Schauer, and Josiah Daniels for your valuable feedback and editorial work. To my students and colleagues at Seattle Pacific University, thanks for being good listeners and conversation partners in the ongoing, often tangential, occasionally unclear verbal processing that is my distracted theological mind. Last, but certainly not least, my journey would have never even started if not for my family, friends, and neighbors in south Seattle and beyond, who have provided me with so many rich experiences and learning opportunities in the day-to-day life of being neighbors and family. I thank God for each of you.

Notes

Introduction: Street Signs and Color Lines

[1]My first book, *Street Signs: Toward a Missional Theology of Urban Cultural Engagement,* is an academic work that explores this idea more fully.

[2]A common stereotype among Asian Americans; see Frank H. Wu, *Yellow: Race in America Beyond Black and White* (New York: Basic Books, 2002), 79.

[3]See Scot McKnight, *A Fellowship of Differents* (Grand Rapids: Zondervan, 2014).

[4]I'll describe examples of these "default postures" in chapter two.

[5]Ta-Nehisi Coates, *Between the World and Me* (New York: Random House, 2015), 10.

1 Theology and Geography

[1]Bill Berry, Peter Buck, Mike Mills, and Michael Stipe, "Stand," *Green,* Warner Bros. Records, 1989.

[2]Ray Bakke, *A Theology as Big as the City* (Downers Grove, IL: InterVarsity Press, 1997), 22-25.

[3]John Rennie Short, *The Urban Order* (Hoboken, NJ: Wiley-Blackwell, 1996), 5.

[4]Karl Barth, on the event of his formal farewell to his students in Bonn just prior to his expulsion from Germany in 1935. Eberhard Busch, *Karl Barth: His Life from Letters and Autobiographical Texts* (Philadelphia: Fortress, 1976).

[5]Kevin J. Vanhoozer, "What Is Everyday Theology?," in Kevin J. Vanhoozer, Charles A. Anderson, and Michael J. Sleasman, *Everyday Theology* (Grand Rapids: Baker Academic, 2007), 18.

[6]Georges Florovsky, *Christianity and Culture* (Belmont, MA: Nordland Publishing, 1974), 67.

[7]Often, "urban" is code language for "black," though its meaning varies widely depending on context.

[8]Willie Jennings, *The Christian Imagination* (New Haven, CT: Yale University Press, 2010), 287-89.

2 Colorblind?

[1]For an accessible primer on this topic, see Mahzarin R. Banaji and Anthony G. Greenwald, *Blindspot: Hidden Biases of Good People* (New York: Delacorte, 2013).

[2]William Faulkner, *Requiem for a Nun* (New York: Random House, 1994), 73.

[3]See Beverly Daniel Tatum, *Why Are All the Black Kids Sitting Together in the Cafeteria?* (New York: Basic Books, 1997).

[4]Geert H. Hofstede, *Cultures and Organizations: Software of the Mind* (New York: McGraw-Hill, 2010), 89-101.

[5]Michael O. Emerson and Christian Smith, *Divided by Faith* (New York: Oxford University Press, 2000), 77.

[6]Ibid., 89.

[7]Ibid.

[8]Reinhold Niebuhr, *Moral Man and Immoral Society* (New York: Simon & Schuster, 1932), 9.

[9]See J. Kameron Carter, *Race: A Theological Account* (New York: Oxford University Press, 2008).

[10]Willie Jennings, *The Christian Imagination* (New Haven, CT: Yale University Press, 2010), 6.

3 From the Garden to the City

[1]Johnny Cash, "No Earthly Good," *The Rambler*, Columbia Records, 1977.

[2]Robert Lupton, "A Theology of Geography," *Urban Mission* 10, no. 4 (1993): 60.

[3]The orphans, widows, and foreigners are a common grouping throughout the Law and Prophets that represent the poor and marginalized. See Deut 10:18; 14:29; 16:11, 14; Jer 7:6; 22:3; Zech 7:10; Mal 3:5.

[4]Harvie Conn and Manuel Ortiz, *Urban Ministry: The Kingdom, the City, and the People of God* (Downers Grove, IL: InterVarsity Press, 2001), 90-91.

[5]Martin Luther King Jr., "Letter from Birmingham Jail," 1963.

[6]Lupton, "Theology of Geography."

4 Walls of Hostility

[1]Nate Silver, "The Most Diverse Cities Are Often the Most Segregated," *FiveThirtyEight*, May 1, 2015, http://fivethirtyeight.com/features/the-most-diverse-cities-are-often-the-most-segregated.

[2]C. C. H. Pounder, Larry Adelman, Jean Cheng, Christine Herbes-Sommers, Tracy Heather Strain, Llewellyn Smith, and Claudio Ragazzi, *Race: The Power of an Illusion* (San Francisco: California Newsreel, 2003).

[3]Rakesh Kochhar and Richard Fry, "Wealth Inequality Has Widened Along Racial, Ethnic Lines Since End of Great Recession," Pew Research Center, December 12, 2014, www.pewresearch.org/fact-tank/2014/12/12/racial-wealth-gaps-great-recession.

[4]Amy Traub and Catherine Ruetschlin, "The Racial Wealth Gap: Why Policy Matters," Dēmos, March 10, 2015, www.demos.org/publication/racial-wealth-gap-why-policy-matters.

[5]Gary Orfield et al., "Brown at 60: Great Progress, a Long Retreat and an Uncertain Future," The Civil Rights Project at UCLA, May 15, 2014, 36, https://civilrightsproject.ucla.edu/research/k-12-education/integration-and-diversity/brown-at-60-great-progress-a-long-retreat-and-an-uncertain-future/Brown-at-60-051814.pdf.

[6]Reed Jordan, "Black Kids' Schools: Segregated by Poverty Too," Real Clear Policy, October 30, 2014, www.realclearpolicy.com/blog/2014/10/30/black_kids_schools_segregated_by_poverty_too_1119.html.

[7]Ibid.

[8]Willie Jennings, *The Christian Imagination* (New Haven, CT: Yale University Press, 2010), 10.

[9]Brenda Salter McNeil, *Roadmap to Reconciliation* (Downers Grove, IL: InterVarsity Press, 2015), 22.

[10]Ibid., 37.

[11]Stanley Hauerwas and William Willimon, *Resident Aliens* (Nashville: Abingdon, 1989), 83.

5 Place, Parish, and Ghetto

[1]Harold Bloom, ed., *Chinua Achebe's Things Fall Apart* (New York: Bloom's Literary Criticism, 2010), 95.

[2]Blue Scholars, "Evening Chai," *Blue Scholars*, 2004.

[3]Janet I. Tu, "Duwamish Tribe Denied Federal Recognition," *The Seattle Times*, July 3, 2015, www.seattletimes.com/seattle-news/puget-sound/duwamish-tribe-denied-federal-recognition.

[4]Aaron Huey, "America's Native Prisoners of War," TEDxDU, September 2010, www.ted.com/talks/aaron_huey.

[5]Ibid.

[6]Chief Seattle Club website, chiefseattleclub.org, accessed July 14, 2016.

[7]Ibid.

[8]Paul Sparks, Tim Soerens, and Dwight J. Friesen, *The New Parish* (Downers Grove, IL: InterVarsity Press, 2014), 23.

[9]Christian Community Development Association, "CCD Philosophy," www.ccda.org/about/ccd-philosophy/listening-to-the-community, accessed August 8, 2016.

[10]Soong-Chan Rah, *Prophetic Lament* (Downers Grove, IL: InterVarsity Press, 2015), 22.

[11]CCDA, "CCD Philosophy."

[12]Douglas S. Massey and Nancy A. Denton, *American Apartheid: Segregation and the Making of the Underclass* (Cambridge, MA: Harvard University Press, 1998), 1.

[13]Michael Harrington, *The Other America: Poverty in the United States* (New York: Touchstone, 1997).

[14]Blaine Kaltman, *Under the Heel of the Dragon: Islam, Racism, Crime, and the Uighur in China* (Athens: Ohio University Press, 2007), 10-11.

6 Gentrification

[1]Mark Greif et al., *What Was the Hipster? A Sociological Investigation* (New York: n+1 Foundation, 2010), x.

[2]Eric Jacobsen, *Sidewalks in the Kingdom: New Urbanism and the Christian Faith* (Grand Rapids: Brazos, 2003), 16.

[3]James Howard Kunstler, *The Geography of Nowhere: The Rise and Decline of America's Man-Made Landscape* (New York: Touchstone, 1993).

[4]John B. Hayes, *Submerge: Living Deep in a Shallow World* (Ventura, CA: Regal Books, 2006), 71.

[5]Ibid., 70.

[6]Kris Rocke and Joel Van Dyke, *Geography of Grace* (Tacoma, WA: Center for Transforming Mission, 2012), 1.

[7]Hayes, *Submerge*, 243.

[8]Malcolm Gladwell, *The Tipping Point: How Little Things Can Make a Big Difference* (New York: Little, Brown, 2000).

[9]Ibid.

[10]Nicole Hannah-Jones, "In Portland's Heart, 2010 Census Shows Diversity

Dwindling," *The Oregonian*, April 30, 2011, www.oregonlive.com/pacific-northwest-news/index.ssf/2011/04/in_portlands_heart_diversity_dwindles.html.

[11]Walter Brueggemann, *The Prophetic Imagination* (Minneapolis: Augsburg Fortress, 2001), 4.

[12]Richard Florida, "The Closest Look Yet at Gentrification and Displacement," *The Atlantic*, November 2, 2015, www.citylab.com/housing/2015/11/the-closest-look-yet-at-gentrification-and-displacement/413356.

7 Reconciliation: A Beautiful (and Disruptive) Story

[1]Michael Polanyi, *Personal Knowledge: Towards a Post-Critical Philosophy* (Chicago: University of Chicago Press, 1958), 53.

[2]Stanley Hauerwas and William Willimon, *Resident Aliens* (Nashville: Abingdon, 1989), 73.

[3]Ibid.

[4]Charles Marsh and John Perkins, *Welcoming Justice* (Downers Grove, IL: InterVarsity Press, 2009), 114.

[5]Ibid., 102.

[6]Cornel West, *The Cornel West Reader* (New York: Civitas Books, 1999), 170.

8 Getting Practical: Action and Reflection

[1]Paulo Freire, *Pedagogy of the Oppressed* (New York: Continuum, 2000).

[2]C. C. H. Pounder, Larry Adelman, Jean Cheng, Christine Herbes-Sommers, Tracy Heather Strain, Llewellyn Smith, and Claudio Ragazzi, *Race: the Power of an Illusion* (San Francisco: California Newsreel, 2003).

[3]Robert P. Jones, "Self-Segregation: Why It's So Hard for Whites to Understand Ferguson," *The Atlantic*, August 21, 2014, www.theatlantic.com/national/archive/2014/08/self-segregation-why-its-hard-for-whites-to-understand-ferguson/378928.

[4]Christena Cleveland, *Disunity in Christ* (Downers Grove, IL: InterVarsity Press, 2013), 74.

[5]Nikole Hannah-Jones, "School Segregation, the Continuing Tragedy of Ferguson," *ProPublica*, December 19, 2014, www.propublica.org/article/ferguson-school-segregation.

[6]Paul Ricoeur, *Interpretation Theory: Discourse and the Surplus of Meaning* (Fort Worth: Texas Christian University Press, 1976), 87.

[7]Bob Ekblad, *Reading the Bible with the Damned* (Louisville, KY: Westminster John Knox, 2005), xvii.

Conclusion: Back to a New Beginning

[1]Grace Lee Boggs, *The Next American Revolution* (Berkeley: University of California Press, 2012), 2, 5.

[2]Ibid., 105.

[3]Ibid., 112.

[4]Ibid., 114.

[5]Ibid., 37.

[6]Ibid., 133-34.

[7]Shane Claiborne, Jonathan Wilson-Hartgrove, and Enuma Okoro, *Common Prayer* (Grand Rapids: Zondervan, 2010), 48.

[8]Willie Jennings, *The Christian Imagination* (New Haven, CT: Yale University Press, 2010), 287-89.

[9]Ibid.